Retention for a Change

PRAISE FOR *RETENTION FOR A CHANGE*

Building a strong team does not happen by accident. Amazing educators across the country pour their hearts and souls into helping their students each and every day. Retaining those amazing educators is important to our profession. As leaders, we need to make sure our teams feel valued. Talk to them, show them your appreciation, and, most of all, let them know you are there to support them every step of the way!

—**Tara Desiderio**, elementary school principal

Every good educational leader recognizes that a school is only as good as the teachers who work there. *Building a Winning Team* is, indeed, mission critical. But as Jones, Vari, and Thomas-EL remind us, "sustaining a winning team" is essential for our schools to thrive. That's why this new book is so important. These authors draw upon research, the wisdom of practitioners in the field, as well as their own experiences to provide "critical tips and tools" for building the type of culture that not just attracts talented educators but keeps them. *Retention for a Change* is not only for administrators, though; it's for any educator who wants to be part of the solution—anyone who wants to contribute to school cultures that energize and inspire.

—**Danny Steele**, educator, author, and speaker

In the Asbury Park School District, under the leadership of our superintendent, Sancha Gray, we are engaging and empowering our learning community through personalized experiences. We promote agency while consistently granting opportunities to all our members. These are all keys to retaining those who have been called to serve and lead. *Retention for a Change* is a wonderful resource for leaders who are looking to invigorate and transform their own school cultures.

—**Laura Brower**, LDT-C, Asbury Park Schools,
"Most Innovative 4 Years in a Row"

In *Retention for a Change*, this amazing author team uncovers a two-part truth to improving our schools and school systems: first, culture supersedes everything else; and second, bringing aboard and keeping high-quality staff is the key to building culture. Education is a people business, and our people matter. A lot. With practical strategies, memorable ideas, and impactful anecdotes, this text provides school leaders with guidance for building and nurturing the team-first, goal-oriented mentality that will lead us to cultivate the schools that our kids deserve.

—**Pete Hall**, former principal and current executive director, EducationHall

As a former principal and now district leader, *Retention for a Change* is a book that I would recommend to all my colleagues. Recruiting and retaining high-quality teachers is a must for any successful administrator, especially today as we face teacher shortages across the nation. The authors have given us a blueprint for building a positive school culture where teachers feel supported and empowered with the tools needed to teach and learn at high levels. I can't wait for you to read *Retention for a Change*.

—**Dr. Rosa Perez-Isiah**, leader for equity, author, presenter

Retention for a Change is an important book for leaders who understand the need to create cultures that support their teachers and staff. The focus of reciprocal investment and a collaborative culture promote self-efficacy within individuals. The authors focus on practitioners who are in the field making an impact and motivating teachers and leaders around the world. Attracting and recruiting talented staff is critical, but retaining positive employees ensures that the success and relationships we build as leaders continue on for decades. I am thankful to the authors for providing such an essential roadmap for all of us, for we are all on this journey toward excellence for students.

—**Bethany Hill**, elementary administrator

Since its inception, Joe and T.J. have led engaging and practical induction programming in Delaware for all new school leaders. Along with Salome, they are influencing positive change in schools across our state. As active practitioners, they bring credibility to the work they lead to improve school leadership. Their new book shares a narrative by practitioners for practitioners on a challenging issue facing leaders across the nation. *Retention for a Change* is precisely the change we need for retention.

—**Michael Saylor**, PhD, Delaware Department of Education

Everyone wants to feel a sense of belonging and purpose in their lives. Educators are no different, and with the constant demands placed on them today, teachers can lose sight of their purpose. *Retention for a Change* helps school leaders remember and reflect upon the influence we have on ensuring that teachers remain tightly aligned to their purpose, and the book calls on leaders to shift our thinking in how to better support our staff. Joe, T.J., and Salome provide clear ideas to be implemented immediately in any school. I highly recommend *Retention for a Change* for a practical approach to teacher retention.

—**Melissa Thomas**, assistant principal,
Dutchtown Middle School

Retention for a Change

Motivate, Inspire, and Energize Your School Culture

Joseph Jones, Salome Thomas-EL,
and T.J. Vari

Foreword by Starr Sackstein

ROWMAN & LITTLEFIELD
Lanham • Boulder • New York • London

Published by Rowman & Littlefield
An imprint of The Rowman & Littlefield Publishing Group, Inc.
4501 Forbes Boulevard, Suite 200, Lanham, Maryland 20706
www.rowman.com

6 Tinworth Street, London SE11 5AL, United Kingdom

British Library Cataloguing in Publication Information Available

Library of Congress Cataloging-in-Publication Data

Library of Congress Control Number: 2020952068

ISBN: 978-1-4758-5882-2 (cloth : alk. paper)
ISBN: 978-1-4758-5883-9 (pbk. : alk. paper)
ISBN: 978-1-4758-5884-6 (electronic)

♾™ The paper used in this publication meets the minimum requirements of
American National Standard for Information Sciences—Permanence of Paper
for Printed Library Materials, ANSI/NISO Z39.48-1992.

Dedication

For this book, our third together, we decided to dedicate it to one educator each, a historical figure or a person from our past, who has transformed our thinking in ways that they will never know.

JOE

As a child, I fell in love with history and became enthralled by the great men and women who stood for what is right and did their part to make this world a better place. When I read *Up from Slavery* by Booker T. Washington, my views on opportunities, education, and the power of our choices were changed forever. In his autobiography, he tells a story of when he tried to enroll in Hampton Institute after an unforgiving journey. Rather than being granted admission, he was asked to sweep the recitation room. Washington didn't hesitate and viewed the request as his entrance exam. He left no doubt in the head teacher's mind that he was meant to be educated there. His struggle to receive a good education and his life's work to educate others has fueled me to provide my students the very best education possible. I'm thrilled I can do that within a career and technical education district.

T.J.

I dedicate this work to Dr. Raymond Theilacker. Dr. Theilacker had a positive and transformational impact on my life and career. Not only was he the best teacher I ever got to observe in the classroom, not only did he make connections with kids from every background imaginable, not only did he teach for more than thirty years, not only did he start what is now considered the most successful teacher institute in the country, not only was he a passionate person about all aspects of life and work, he was a dear friend. He impacted my life, my daily work, my sense of efficacy, and my philosophical outlook on much of what I do, from teaching to learning to leading. I miss him every single day. Rest in peace, my friend. You will always be missed.

SALOME

My thirty-three years of work in the inner-city in Philadelphia, PA, and Wilmington, DE, have been influenced and inspired by Mrs. Marva Collins who was born in 1936, the same year as my mother, and raised in Alabama. Mrs. Collins moved to Chicago early in her teaching career. She spent years as a substitute teacher, and then started the Westside Preparatory School, using money from her own savings account, to help low-income inner-city students in Chicago. The school was located in her home and survived for over thirty years. Early in my teaching career, my mother and I began a Saturday Learning Academy in her home where inner-city students could receive extra academic help and a good home-cooked meal. Many of those students went on to do very well in school, with some receiving bachelor's and master's degrees in college. This book is dedicated to Marva Collins, a true education hero!

Contents

Foreword

Starr Sackstein

Invest in the people you hire if you want them to be ambassadors of your department, school, or district. That may sound simple, but too many organizations need help with this and *Retention for a Change* spells it out for school leaders.

If almost twenty years as an educator has taught me anything, it 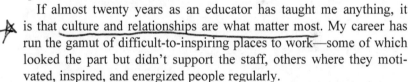 is that culture and relationships are what matter most. My career has run the gamut of difficult-to-inspiring places to work—some of which looked the part but didn't support the staff, others where they motivated, inspired, and energized people regularly.

Early in my career, before I knew longevity was going to happen, there were instructional leaders who saw something special in me. Opportunities to develop my craft and investments in me as a person happened both privately and publicly. Since I was eager to be better than just okay, I worked hard to keep improving with their support, despite the inherent challenges that exist for early career teachers. It was because of this early foundational support that I felt able to take risks, knowing that mistakes would be made and that from those mistakes necessary growth would happen. That's the investment that needs to be made in every new teacher if we want them to grow into masters.

Building the right relationship with the place you work has the ability to make or break your everyday life. If you're in the wrong school, if it's a bad fit, teaching can be an absolute struggle. When you are in the right place, where your values and beliefs align, then work doesn't have to feel like work. It can be invigorating. This symbiotic relationship works on both sides. And as educational leaders, we have an obligation to our colleagues and teammates to do the best we can to lift each other up.

As opportunities arose, my career took me in a different direction. There was a specialized school that really felt like it could be the right fit for me. The hiring process was a tiring one and not because I had to come back three times and jump through the usual hoops. When my interview was set up, they requested I spend the whole day there.

It was explained that I would teach a lesson, speak with students and staff, and hang out to see if it was a good fit. The extra length they went in hiring the right people definitely mattered. It meant finding great teachers and then retaining them because everyone had a say; that was evident right from the start.

My day on-site went so well that by the end of it, the principal was pouring over my portfolio and having letters written to offer me the position. It was clear that they wanted me and I wanted them. It felt good to be wanted and I was excited to take on the new role at this school. I'd be able to use my new journalism knowledge and develop a program of my own as head of the print newspaper path the school was planning to build.

We functioned with the understanding that we were building the plane while it was flying, which meant things wouldn't be perfect right away and that was okay, as long as we kept improving. That's what we get when everyone is on the same page, operating from a growth mindset.

The school felt like home.

For the first few years, I worked tirelessly to help improve the school, build my program, and contribute to student success. I was well-respected among my colleagues, appreciated by my leaders, and loved and respected by my students. But, as the school grew, the attention to detail that was paid to hiring the folks waned, and after five years, the school felt like any other school might feel. The original culture was no longer recognizable. This is why what these authors offer in their books, *Building a Winning Team* and, now, *Retention for a Change*, is so important; they address a culture of retention. They explore why hiring matters so much and what we need to be doing to sustain cultures of growth, even after years of being in the same place.

Rather than stay and allow the growing toxic environment to spoil the feelings I had about being in the classroom, I started looking elsewhere. That's the problem with cultures that don't support the teaching staff; they leave. I landed in another high school in the position of a lifetime as a teacher center facilitator and instructional coach, which allowed me to be in the classroom and work with teachers simultaneously.

Professionally, this was the direction I had hoped to move in for years and I was excited to be empowered in it. All of the leaders I worked with were supportive and I was involved in everything. My voice mattered. The work we were doing mattered and the opportunity to start building was evident. Not only was I inspired and energized, I was giving my all and so were the people around me.

Building relationships with educators, colleagues, students, and community is hard work, but it is absolutely essential if we want to make change and maintain the teams we build. In the different roles I've held, I've had the capacity to learn the goals of the folks on my team and then empower them in different ways. One teacher, toward the end of her classroom teaching career, wanted to write a book and we worked together to make that happen. A few particularly talented and innovative teachers wanted to go to a national conference and present, and so we made that happen.

When teachers asked to attend professional learning experiences outside of the district, I did what I could to support their goals. If they wanted to try the things they learned in those trainings, I supported their efforts because it matters. It gave us all purpose and it made us happy. Teachers want to feel like what they do is making a difference, not just with the kids but in their schools and in their communities. We have the power to help them feel appreciated in whatever ways they want to be. Getting to know them to be able to do that effectively takes time, but is worth it. Doing so creates the culture of a winning team and develops the mindset that we're all members of it.

As I read *Retention for a Change*, I found myself agreeing audibly with its tenets. As school leaders, on every level, we have an obligation to create environments that both attract the right people for our organizations and then retain them once they accept a position. This is a career that takes vigilance and this book will help make this sometimes daunting job possible.

It is evident from three distinct stories of my career—I've been supported as a new teacher, I've felt alone as someone trying to contribute my best, and I've been energized in a culture of ownership and empowerment. It's amazing how several critical aspects of our workplace can make or break our working experience.

Throughout the easily readable pages of this book, you will learn ways to amplify what you are doing that works and to add new strategies that will lead to a better culture in your school or district, the kind that people talk about and that attracts new talent. It's a cycle of change that's needed in schools to retain teachers. It's the change we need in education and this book gets it right.

Joe, Salome, and T. J. will challenge you to reflect on your current practices and encourage you to try out some of the new techniques they offer. Be honest with yourself and make the appropriate changes so that your school truly is the kind of place where your employees enjoy coming to work. Happy educators are the best ambassadors for a school community. They share their stories on social media, they participate in the lives of their students, and they openly communicate about what is working and what can continue to improve for the betterment of everyone.

Retention for a Change will be the first step in a series of professional moves that is sure to improve the lives of all of the people in your district. And, have fun with it.

—Starr Sackstein, author of *Hacking Assessment*
and many other books for educators, speaker,
consultant, and former high school teacher
and instructional coach

Preface

This book was written to complement our *Building a Winning Team* (*BWT*) book, which focused on creating a magnetic reputation and actively recruiting the best teachers for your school and district. The critical notion is that hiring practices need to be separated into three distinct phases—*before* you hire, *during* hiring, and *after* you hire.

We argue that hiring practices in schools are somewhat elusive, focusing on seasonal issues with turnover, confusing our practice of recruitment for retention, and falling short of building the team you need for a better school. We have experienced the reactive nature of schools when it comes to filling positions and retaining staff, and we're flipping that conversation for you and your team.

But *BWT* only addressed *before* and *during* hiring, leaving much to be said about retention (*after* you hire). In our "BDA R3 Model," the *before*, *during*, and *after* (BDA) are *reputation*, *recruitment*, and *retention* (R3). Through research and writing, though, we found that retention deserved its own book and so we publish this work as a sequel to *BWT*.

Of course, this book can be read on its own. The details, descriptions, explanations, stories, and tips are all sound practices that need not be prefaced by *BWT*. That said, they complement each other in a way that offers balance for school leaders seeking a new lens for the totality of their hiring practices.

Here, in *Retention for a Change*, we address the desperate need for a change in school culture. Our audience includes district leaders, directors of human resources, school leaders, teacher leaders, and public officials who see the need for stronger retention practices in schools so that we're no longer losing our best people to other school systems. Although the grass is rarely greener on the other side of the fence, it can appear that way when the going gets tough, which it almost always does at some point during each school year.

The ideas herein will help you to grow greener grass, to keep it green when droughts set in, and to improve the health of every blade so that the grass on your side of the fence is always finer to gaze upon and a better place to learn and play than any other nearby pastures.

Allow us to introduce you to some of the key features that you'll find as you read. In the introduction, we make the case that retention is the change we need in schools, not the other way around. Focusing on retention is a cultural shift, and when we do what it takes to support our staff, they stay. That's what it means to change a culture from within.

We also revisit our fable school, Pembroke, one last time as an explicit reference to *Building a Winning Team*. Chapter 1 opens our discussion by defining what we call the *Retention Accelerators*. When motivation, inspiration, and energy flow freely within your organization, you'll find greater success as well as a sense of satisfaction in our daily work. Chapter 1 also includes a deep dive into some of the problems and solutions with titles, pay, and professional development for educators.

Chapters 2, 3, and 4 are structured to address all three of the *Retention Accelerators*—motivation, inspiration, and energy. Each of these three chapters comes with a "Practitioner Spotlight" to introduce you to a story about some of our heroes, in the field, doing the work. And, each comes with a "Technical Tip" that will help you to create the change you need in your school or district so that retention is no longer an issue. You'll find models to use, mindsets to shift, and masters to emulate.

The last two chapters of the book are entirely dedicated to new teachers, although the practices we discuss are still about culture and engagement for everyone in your school. It's important to note that when we refer to "new teachers," we're not only talking about new teachers to the profession but also new teachers to your building. New people, in general, need to be treated differently, regardless of their years of experience in the field. These last two chapters reveal a story about ownership and commitment, called Standing Out. You won't be disappointed. And, they also each include a "Leadership Team Activity" for your school to implement.

Finally, the conclusion is all about cultivating what we call a "membership mentality." Rather than treating people as employees, we make the case for developing a culture of membership instead. Each of the primary six chapters have "Guiding Questions" to promote reflection and evaluation based on the concepts we present.

Acknowledgments

We would like to acknowledge career educators—those who have made education their life's work. We admire everyone who has spent their career working in this field for the betterment of children and communities. Although there are those who choose to leave early, and some who leave and come back, we know that the vast majority of educators spend their entire lives serving children. Education, teaching in particular, is a calling. You can't do it for twenty-five, thirty, or thirty-five-plus years if you don't feel the passion for this work from your inner core. We acknowledge anyone who has paved the way in this noble field so that others can be inspired by their stories and commitment to such important work.

Introduction

We aptly named this book *Retention for a Change* for two reasons: 1) We firmly believe that our cultures in schools and school systems must change so that retention is no longer the problem that it is today in education, and 2) We have found in our own experiences that retention strategies themselves can actually prompt a change in culture. In other words, in our efforts to engage with new and different strategies to retain our best staff, we change the culture toward what it should be to retain them in the first place.

When we published *Building a Winning Team: The Power of a Magnetic Reputation and the Need to Recruit Top Talent in Every School* (*BWT*), we already had this book in mind. In fact, we released *BWT* first because we did not want to confuse readers into thinking that motivation for your workforce is what helps to build a winning team. To "build," you need to begin *before* you have a vacancy and *during* the active recruitment phases of your team's formation. Too many "culture" books fail to recognize that great teams aren't born from a great culture but, rather, built through reputation, recruitment, and fine-tuning a culture that motivates, inspires, and energizes its workforce.

We are somehow led to believe that if we come on board as new leaders and we simply employ culture-building tactics, our schools will transform into places of wonder and amazement. The reality is that this is only partially true, and it ignores the need to build your team from without and within through vision, virtue, communication, engagement, and fanfare. Great leaders are builders; they build teams that win.

But team culture needs constant attention. Even the greatest teams need care (Gordon, 2018). That's why this book is so important because it delves into all of the critical tips and tools for sustaining a winning team. With the right focus and attention, leaders can alter their team's workplace experiences and expectations forever.

So much of what we know about the human condition is new. A growing body of research is emerging with loads of information about social psychology, human potential, and how our brains work. But we have found that not nearly enough of this new information is being used for employee motivation and retention, and there's a serious deficit in how we employ this new learning in education. We are only scratching the surface of what it means to have a highly engaged teacher work-force, an inspired professional atmosphere, and an energizing environment in schools. With this book, we dive deeper than ever before into how to apply these concepts as school and district leaders.

Even schools that have learned to focus on their best teachers first (Whitaker, 2012), rather than working to motivate the lowest performers (Clark, 2015), are in need of the strategies you'll find in this book. We believe that you'll find some of our content practical with an immediate translation to action, but other aspects of what we offer are esoteric, abstract, and even sublime. The reason for that is because schools, and any workplace for that matter, can be places of magic, glory, and zeal.

What we've uncovered through experience and research is that work is far more psychological, cerebral, and emotional than it is physical, industrious, or burdensome. When we reshape our thinking to focus on the *meta* aspects of teaching and learning, we begin to see that motivation, inspiration, and energy are the true work of a masterful school leader.

RETAINING YOUR BEST TEACHERS: MOTIVATION, INSPIRATION, AND ENERGY

Retaining effective employees is a global issue that affects all industries. Whether employees believe that management is dishonest and lacks integrity (Covey, 2006), perceive that there's simply a limit to potential opportunities for growth in the company (Johnson, 2018), or feel that they are more like a commodity than a person, people leave companies that they believe have inadequate support, poor communication, or disjointed goals and purpose.

In *Lead from the Heart* (2011), Mark Crowley recounts a common and difficult situation. When he took over as a manager, he was met with resentment and outright resistance. Interestingly, the main ringleader of the negativity never even worked with Mark, yet he conceived of and communicated Mark's ineffectiveness to others and even to superiors within the company. The powerful lesson from this story is that this individual's fears and beliefs were based on an experience that he had with one of Mark's former colleagues. Mark was merely guilty by association.

Mark didn't become vindictive or seek to fire the person. By all other accounts, this employee was good. Rather than fueling her misguided perception, he built a personal relationship with her and, over time, they developed a strong and healthy working relationship. Mark understood that leading a committed and effective staff is a long, and sometimes lonely, path, taking several different turns and it is often very bumpy along the way.

Past situations and experiences can haunt current realities, whether justified or not. And unfortunately they can impact overall organizational effectiveness and employee retention. Mark's story helps us to see the big picture. Effective leaders work to empower their employees and seek out several avenues to lead people. They help them discover their own uniqueness and contribution within the organization to create independence and cohesion.

Engaged and motivated staff take ownership of their professional well-being and growth; develop a deeper connection with their students, their school, and their community; and stay at their school for the long haul because they know that they are making a difference. By recognizing how each person contributes to and fits into the overall purpose of the organization, we can inspire teachers to give their best effort and reach new heights. The culture itself will unleash the energy to do so.

Although teacher turnover is a real problem for schools, we contend that there are a number of culture-building strategies that can combat the issue. There are a variety of reasons that impact teacher attrition, which we explore throughout the book, but what we do know is that retaining teachers and creating stability are critical for student achievement and maximizing progress.

This requires an ongoing, concerted effort among administrators—at both the school and district levels—to support teachers, to offer good working conditions, and to empower them by giving them a voice. Tackling teacher retention is arguably the first step in reducing the burden on the overall system, and "addressing early attrition is critical to stemming the country's continuing shortage crisis" (Carver-Thomas & Darling-Hammond, 2016).

Understanding the factors that contribute to the reasons why teachers are leaving, who is most likely to leave, and under what conditions teachers will likely leave, provides the basis for concrete answers. Every school and school system is different, with many variables contributing to success or failure, but one initial step in the right direction for all of us is having insight into how to proactively address retention through motivation, inspiration, and energy at work.

Teacher retention is a growing concern, particularly in our most difficult schools. The underlying challenges that schools face must be met with strong networks, better support systems, and unique alliances, both within the school and throughout the community. Whether it is building strong professional communities that support collegial growth (Johnson, Berg, & Donaldson, 2005) or developing systems that offer career advancement for teachers while still keeping them in the classroom, there are best practices and possible solutions.

In the following pages, we delve into many of the success practices that will work in your school as you begin to better support your new staff and develop the current people on your team. We wrote this book to introduce the key strategies for how to retain your teachers within three important areas that schools must leverage:

1. Teacher motivation stems from meaningful engagement in their work and deep connections to the purpose of it. First, we must leverage motivation and a personal desire to engage.
2. Inspiration comes from a feeling that we're doing generous, connected work. Second, we must leverage what it means to inspire people to be their best.
3. Energized working environments are focused on employee well-being and their enthusiasm for doing important tasks. Third, we must leverage energy by taking ownership and modeling the way.

These critical steps to a motivated and quality workforce are alive within our ability to invest in them as people and professionals. Before we get started with the *Retention Accelerators* in Chapter 1, let's be reminded of the power in a great working culture through the story of Pembroke High School.

PEMBROKE HIGH SCHOOL

When the new biotech teacher, Suzanne, started teaching in the fall at Pembroke High to begin and grow the new program, with no traditional educational experience under her belt, the principal knew that she would require a strong network of support to survive. Her industry credentials were incredibly impressive and, along with her science background, she even had a Juris Doctor degree with a concentration in patent law.

She was a tremendous force of knowledge, energy, and excitement. The leadership team was ecstatic with their new recruit. Many wondered why she would leave an incredible position in her current company to teach at Pembroke, but after twenty-seven successful years at a leading biotech firm, she wanted something new from her work and thought that teaching would be an incredible way to give back. She hoped to inspire high school students to love the subject matter like she did.

As anticipated, the months of October and November were beginning to weigh on Suzanne. She was no stranger to long days and late nights, but the classroom can be an incredible drain on even the most impressive teachers. Not only was Suzanne saddled with the responsibility of starting a new program, she also had to fulfill some course requirements to earn a teaching certificate. She felt herself going in every direction.

She was essentially creating a brand new program with no viable curriculum, plus she was trying to master the art of teaching, learning the craft while practicing it for the first time. Although most days felt more like survival than mastery, she was managing all of the ancillary responsibilities associated with teaching, such as attending meetings, calling parents, and staying after school with students. It was definitely a whirlwind of an experience, but she liked it.

Fortunately, the Pembroke principal foresaw many of these challenges and knew that a strong network of support was crucial for Suzanne's success. The last thing that the school could afford was for Suzanne to quit. Knowing the early trials of any teacher, let alone someone pursuing an alternative route to certification, the principal instituted several key supports. The groundwork of the support system was established by ensuring that Suzanne wasn't isolated. With formal opportunities to meet other staff members and build relationships, she made connections that protected her from the remote feeling that new teachers can get on bad days.

The next level of support happened through the culture of the school. The principal found simple and specific ways to energize the staff, offer praise that reinforced the school's mission, and genuinely appreciate everyone's hard work. This specific praise for Suzanne's work seemed to come when she needed it the most.

Lastly, Suzanne had a dynamo of a mentor. Her mentor was an English language arts teacher with twelve years of experience at the school. She was an expert in all things teaching and a remarkable instructor in the classroom. Soft-spoken among her colleagues and very judicious with her words, she utterly transformed when she was in front of her students. She was a master, and Suzanne gained loads of advice and encouragement by watching her teach and consulting her when planning.

All of these efforts paid serious dividends. Despite Suzanne's exhaustion and heavy lift, she never felt alone. Yes, she had to design the curriculum from scratch for a new program at the school, but her mentor helped provide models and templates to organize the work. She loved the school. Her career in biotech was very rewarding, but she felt at home in her new role. The fact that the school culture was so uplifting only reminded her of her goal to be an awesome teacher and inspire students to love the content.

Last, but certainly not of any lesser significance to her classroom accomplishments, the staff socials, planned by a dedicated group of teacher leaders, gave her an opportunity to discuss work, share stories, and gain a deep connection with Pembroke High through collegiality and meaningful friendships. She knew that she was growing professionally and building relationships, which motivated and inspired her to put forth her best effort for her new team.

We use the story of Pembroke to illustrate a culture where staff are motivated, inspired, and energized to be their best and give their all. Suzanne is new, but she's also valued and supported. The system keeps her lifted, happy, and even healthy as she makes her contribution to the team. When things seem bleak, she knows she's not alone. That's what happens when all three of the *Retention Accelerators* are at work.

Chapter One

Learning to Lift

Too many organizations—not just companies but governments and nonprofits as well—still operate from assumptions about human potential and individual performance that are outdated, unexamined, and rooted more in folklore than in science (Pink, 2009, p. 9).

THE RETENTION ACCELERATORS

The three most important drivers of a successful organization are its ability to *motivate, inspire,* and *energize* the workforce. We call these the *Retention Accelerators* because when all three are equally at play, employees feel supported, celebrated, and happy. Yes, even "happy" at work. This begins with the leader's commitment to making an ongoing investment in the staff.

Interestingly, though, this investment is a process and, although not incredibly complicated, it gets misconstrued, overlooked, and even rejected within many organizations. In education, our lack of investment in teachers has resulted in the issues we have with retaining them. Without motivation, inspiration, and energy infused into our school cultures, we can create cultures devoid of the investments we need to make for people to feel and be effective.

By not lifting and growing our teachers adequately, we can inadvertently hold them back, limiting the necessary resources to do the job effectively and inhibiting their development as professionals. The outcome is disengagement at work and low morale, among other negative consequences. The good news is that much of this is well within an effective leader's control. By taking an interest in our people and their growth, we improve their capacity and increase their gratification at work.

"We could improve productivity [too] if we stopped systematically underinvesting in human capital" (Garton, 2017). It would be better if we were starting from a neutral point, but we're actually working from below the ground floor. Years of underinvestment in teachers is going to require a major lift. We must now begin to work within a model of strategic investment. To do so, the first step is to understand the forces that are working against us, creating the inverted investment model that we currently have in education.

In *Building a Winning Team* we detailed the power in telling a positive story about your school and the need for unique and highly effective hiring practices to recruit better teachers; the next piece of the puzzle is to create meaningful engagement at work so that you don't lose them. This loss is experienced in two ways: 1) A reduction in effort and commitment to the work, and/or 2) A literal loss of teachers to other schools and districts that they believe will appreciate their contributions. This is why the *before*, *during*, and *after* formula for building a winning team is so important. The *before* and *during* take place when we are strategically assembling our team, and the *after* is what great leaders know and do once the team is in place.

The reality is that highly functioning teams need ongoing support and development to perform at their best. Mankins and Garton (2017) report that great companies, with the right focus on unleashing critical aspects of productivity, have up to 40 percent greater output than the competition. For schools, that translates to better student engagement and increased performance in the classroom.

This is precisely why employee motivation must be viewed as a retention strategy. The problem is that many systems are failing in their efforts to retain quality teachers. This is happening, in part, because many human resource strategies are geared towards recruitment efforts and lack the necessary retention practices for staff to feel connected to the culture.

Let's start with money. Money is a great way to initially attract prospective hires, but people stay at their schools because of a deep connection and sense of belonging. Monetary incentives, although used as retention tactics, are not effective as such when they're not coupled with other improvements. Of course money is a factor, and we'll tackle it later in our "Deeper Dive," but it's not a driving force on its own. Employees stay for the long haul when the leader's actions demonstrate a commitment to a quality environment. Retention is not the result of an incentive, like money, but rather the outcome when people are engaged. It's the day-to-day connections between the people and the work that matter most.

The fact is that people don't quit their jobs, they quit their direct manager. And although it's a mere cliché to claim this as the truth, it's something to understand better for the sake of what happens when we don't lead people effectively. To explain this reality, we need to uncover the reasons *why* people quit their manager, especially when they might otherwise believe in their work. New research provides a rationale at a much more granular level, adding clarity to what it means to be disgruntled on the job and why certain industries are experiencing high turnover.

In one study, job quitters who cited management as the issue indicated that the manager's performance, not their management practices, was the main reason. The study revealed that 40 percent of people who rated their supervisor as a poor performer also interviewed for another job in the previous three months of their employment (Schwantes, 2018).

It's revealing to discover that engagement is not just the result of how the supervisor manages people but also how she contributes to the team as a fellow worker. Further exploration reveals that the top "management" issues that resulted in turnover include lack of recognition, company culture, inadequate growth opportunities, long hours, and boredom in their role (Schwantes, 2018; Fisher, 2018). Fortunately, these issues are manageable, and they begin with investing in people to increase and maintain their engagement through motivation, inspiration, and energy. In Chapters 2, 3 and 4, we tackle each one separately to show you how you can create an environment that your winning team deserves.

All told, the answer to our retention problems can be summed up in three words: meaningful employee engagement. This may seem reductionist, considering the multifaceted nature of the issue. However, when teachers are engaged in their classroom, school, and community, they value their work and appreciate their jobs. This results in a deeper connection with the school community, which leads to a much longer tenure in their roles.

The key is in understanding *how* leaders create this environment for their employees. Identifying such a complex issue and tangentially addressing it with generalities is no different than simply pointing the finger at "managers" as the reason for all of our work culture issues. To truly begin to understand engagement at work requires far more dissection and analysis.

First, engagement can look and sound different among the various job functions within a school. This means that understanding the intricacies at play for each individual is fundamental when looking to improve employee retention. In fact, "engagement could represent job satisfaction, emotional investment in the cause, willingness to invest discretionary effort, or advocating for the company as a good place to work" (Fuller & Shikaloff, 2017). A deeper account of what it means to be engaged is a pivotal first step because engagement likely means something different to everyone.

Second, school leaders must be cautious that their employee engagement efforts are not caught up in fighting against dissatisfaction versus actively building an environment of genuine commitment. Too often, a leader's day is totally consumed by issues and problems. They end up falling into the trap of believing that successfully managing and putting out fires is the same as lifting and growing teachers. This leads to an undercurrent that the administration's role is to handle every concern as it arises rather than to spend time to proactively develop others so that the team is working together to resolve school matters. This only preoccupies the leader, diverting her attention away from creating a culture of engagement by working to quell the frustrations of the day.

Third, even when we focus on "employee satisfaction" as a norm, our approach isn't strong enough to retain top talent. Research reveals that "satisfied" employees feel safe, have the tools, training, and resources to do their jobs, are able to work efficiently without bureaucratic tape, and feel valued and rewarded (Garton & Mankins, 2015). Compare that to "engaged" employees who enjoy teamwork, autonomy, growth, and impact. And then make the comparison again to "inspired" employees who find meaning at work (Garton & Mankins, 2015). School leaders need to effectively blend a feeling of safety and value with higher levels of inspiration, included only in the aspects of work that provide autonomy and meaning to every employee.

Employees who work in an organization that fosters meaning through each person's role enjoy the greatest sense of job satisfaction as well as personal fulfillment and self-actualization. Engaged, self-actualized employees are always striving "to reach their highest potential" within their unique contribution to the team (Gostick & Elton, 2007, p. 59). This is the reason why we start our discussion with "the right resources" and "career development" as fundamental to lifting and growing your people.

If people are equipped with the best tools, developed in their roles, motivated to excel, inspired by the mission, and energized by the outcomes, you'll engage employees and move them along the continuum of satisfaction, inspiration, fulfillment, and self-actualization. And, when the school culture exists at the highest level of engagement, retaining teachers is no longer an issue.

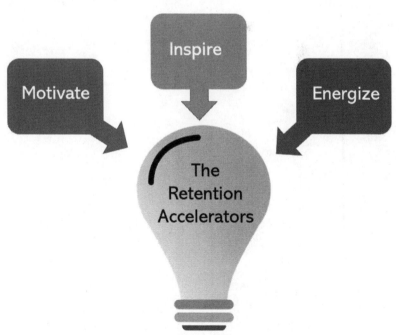

Figure 1.1.   The Retention Accelerators Model. Image created by author.

The Right Resources

On the spectrum of employee satisfaction, at the lowest level, staff are at least equipped with the essential tools and resources to do their jobs (Garton & Mankins, 2015). Yet it is well-known, and unfairly accepted as normal, that teachers spend a considerable amount of their own money on supplies for students, so much so that our federal government allows for a tax deduction for those who itemize what they spend on classroom resources.

In fact, in the beginning of the 2019 school year, many teachers took to Twitter as a cry for help with the hashtag #clearthelist to identify items that they needed in their classrooms, hoping that people would purchase supplies from their lists on Amazon. Items ranged from disinfectant wipes to storybooks. As an industry, we are essentially acquiescing to the fact that our people must improve their own situations and tolerate working conditions that don't meet a simple standard for job satisfaction.

But beyond the mere supplies to do be able to do the work, teachers need resources that meet the needs of their students. In our *Passionate Leadership* book, we noted the need for "the right resources" in schools (Thomas-EL, Jones, & Vari, 2020). By "right" we mean two things: 1) Too often, the resources that are allocated to schools are misaligned with the actual student learning deficits or the teachers' understanding of *how* and *why* to use the tools that are available, and 2) Teachers and programs often need resources that can be accessed more easily than we think.

First, small and large school systems alike purchase programs and resources that either don't match the learning targets of their students or don't get used adequately. We're not implying intentional excess or waste but rather a misunderstanding of the necessary environment requirements and resources that are needed for teacher and student success. This happens when programs are implemented without the associated professional development necessary to use the tools with fidelity, when teachers are given less than adequate access to curriculum, and when teachers don't completely understand how a given tool aligns to the fulfillment of its associated need.

One way to combat this problem is by using three steps that are a function of the school level leadership team: 1) Conduct a thorough needs analysis to identify the root cause of a problem, 2) Communicate the problem-of-practice to the key stakeholders, and 3) Define the purpose that a new resource fulfills in solving the problem.

Consider ninth grade mathematics as an example of how to solve a need by using data to effectively identify and manage the problem. In this scenario, students aren't performing well on the eleventh grade Preliminary SAT/National Merit Scholarship Qualifying Test. The leader must gather key people around the table to analyze the issue by reviewing the data to better understand why the students are underperforming. Consequently, the team discovers gaps in what the College Board identifies as the "Heart of Algebra" and, in particular, linear equations.

The Heart of Algebra comprises a large portion of the assessment so when an analysis uncovers an area of need, it's critical to communicate a clear problem-of-practice (an area that needs immediate attention) to gain further clarity of that issue. We cannot assume that everyone will understand the reasons behind the low student performance, which is the rationale for the ongoing analysis. Even so, not everyone is likely to be at the table for the discovery, which is another reason why we communicate the problem as widely as possible.

As such, we must cultivate statements like "the problem is that students aren't scoring at proficiency in the area of algebraic reasoning." This step is important because we often focus on the problem and not the symptoms. Within our scenario, to help improve the eleventh grade PSAT scores, we actually need to look into our ninth grade math curriculum because that is where algebra is typically taught. A thorough analysis tells us more about where to implement the solution, not just that the problem itself exists.

Knowing where to spend our time and add support is as important as having the right resources in the first place. In this case, implementing a new resource or program at the eleventh grade level will not improve student scores, which only adds to the frustration about both the scores and the constant barrage of curriculum changes.

Next, we need to define the purpose of our new program and how it will help solve the problem. Suppose the team decides to use Khan Academy to remediate the gaps identified in the data analysis. It's a free resource and, according to Khan, 20 hours of studying on their "Official SAT Practice" leads to an average gain of 115 points on the exam (Khan Academy, 2017). Thus, our purpose for using Khan may sound something like this: "If students practice using Khan activities that are directly linked to their personal deficits for a minimum of 20 hours, specifically honing in on algebraic reasoning, they will improve their understanding of the concept and improve their scores."

This might seem simplistic, but the target of 20 hours and the specificity of the area of focus provides a level of clarity that can be measured by the students' overall progress. Too often, programs are implemented without very clear goals. Couple that with poor communication and a vague understanding of why Khan Academy is the chosen initiative and the staff may view it as "one more thing," resulting in minimal compliance at best.

Clear messaging is vital to the success of the initiative as it creates greater awareness among the staff and provides an overall rationale. Teachers desire to understand the purpose of the program, how it's going to be implemented, and ultimately why it's important. If school leaders are encountering teachers who are not using the resources or are finding a misalignment between the identified needs of the students and the program, it's usually due to a lack of communication and understanding.

Mandated compliance, misaligned programming, and poor communication are what we dub as the *Teacher Alienators*—the complete opposite to the *Retention Accelerators*—aspects of work that cause unnecessary doubt, fear, and uncertainty. These problems are exactly what teachers cite when they leave a school or the profession.

It's too easy to argue that we don't have the right tools to do our jobs effectively when, in many circumstances, much of the problem lies within the misunderstanding of how to attack a problem and the best method of communicating its resolution. As this continues over lengthy periods of time, teachers can grow weary, producing a negative perception toward the work and a belief that they are not supported with the appropriate resources to be effective—both of which detract from job satisfaction and employee engagement in schools.

Second, schools need to fully leverage the available resources that are often at our fingertips. It comes down to the consistent use of sites like Khan Academy and the plethora of free online solutions available. The internet has opened a world of resources for schools to use and engage students in dynamic ways to support learning. In the digital era, and the one-to-one movement, schools and teachers are getting better at accessing free online tools and resources.

The accessibility to shared documents that the Google platform offers provides teachers with a fundamental avenue to expand their world and connect with others well beyond their own walls to improve teaching and learning. And these aren't the only tools without a fee for use. Many universities, federal and state agencies, parks and recreational facilities, nonprofits, and even nearby businesses have free services that might support any given unit of study within the classroom.

Casting a wide net and shifting our thinking to *how we want students to experience the content* and *how it will connect them to the real world* is a powerful way to plan lessons. Schools that facilitate the use of outside resources are able to inspire and motivate teachers to think "outside the box." And, when teachers consistently create engaging and fresh experiences for their students, they engage with the work in a way that transforms how they see their role. Instead of content creator or lesson facilitator, they can become world explorer and "ah-ha moment" provider. This helps to spark a new interest in our courses and careers so that we approach our craft with enthusiasm and curiosity versus stagnation and status quo.

When employees have the resources and tools to do their jobs effectively, especially when resources are flowing and directly connected to student learning, satisfaction is guaranteed. As we consider the use of new tools and resources to satisfy the workforce through deeper engagement, we must also consider how we develop the workforce as they grow along a career continuum. It's not until every teacher feels like they have the right resources available to them and a career path that supports their development that we can begin to build our culture of motivation, inspiration, and energy.

Career Development

In a research study regarding retention, employees who stay in their jobs "found their work enjoyable 31% more often, used their strengths 33% more often, and expressed 37% more confidence that they were gaining skills and experiences they need to develop their careers" (Goler, Gale, Harrington, & Grant, 2018). Education has long used *professional development* (PD) as the standard nomenclature for on-the-job learning or training that teachers receive to improve their performance. Unfortunately, the standards are generally low in this area. In fact, in our experiences, teachers are often loathe to participate in professional development, not because they don't want to learn but because the format is typically less than engaging.

We want to shift the thinking from *professional development* toward *career development* for two important reasons: 1) To retain teachers, we must invest in their growth throughout their careers by evaluating and identifying success as more than years of service, and 2) To retain teachers, we must support their growth and development throughout their careers in the classroom in a way that mirrors their needs and evolves over time to support new learning. These two shifts are drastic changes to the current mindset around a career in teaching.

The first considers a multitiered approach to how we view the role of a teacher—whereby teachers can be in different categories within the same role and different job descriptions based on that role—rather than using years of service or degrees earned as the sole indicators of where they are in their careers.

The second requires us to think about teacher development in a new way. Because teachers experience learning on the continuum of their service trajectory, they should be valued for their expertise, not just their time. We go into greater detail regarding what this looks like in the following "Deeper Dive."

DEEPER DIVE: TEACHER TITLES, PAY SCALES, AND MICRO-CREDENTIALING

As we stated before, a new approach and a new philosophy to *professional development* requires us to think about teachers in terms of *career development*, and two prominent areas must be addressed to start: 1) To retain teachers, we must support and recognize their growth throughout their careers, considering stages of advancement and distinction rather than years of service, and 2) A different approach to professional learning and credentialing will require schools to strategically invest in their teachers, which will lead to greater expertise as well as retention. In other words, teachers need career development structures to differentiate the advancements that they make on a continuum of their service, and they need ongoing professional learning experiences that build on their expertise.

Teacher effectiveness and motivation cannot be left to one-and-done evaluation systems and salary schedules that are based solely on time. These two shifts in practice require a new approach to teacher evaluation, which may include changes in state codes, teacher contracts, and even laws. Fortunately, some states already allow districts to submit alternative evaluation tools for greater alignment to the vision and philosophy of the local education system.

Regardless, we need more flexibility in the way we meet the needs of our teachers, and it will likely come with resistance. However, this cannot stop us from tackling such an important problem, one that threatens teacher retention and job satisfaction.

This first shift doesn't necessarily mean a change in pay structures, although it can and arguably should. Regardless, starting small and building from there would be prudent and wise. What it does require, though, is a shift in the way we support and evaluate teachers for growth. We don't advocate for an evaluation system that ties teacher pay to performance indicators like annual test scores, but we do see the need for structural changes in current salary scales.

The first change we're proposing is that teachers get "credit" for all of their roles in school and not just that of "teacher." In *Passionate Leadership* (2020), we called for title distinctions for every teacher, with particular distinction for those who serve in roles that go above and beyond the classroom to support the overall functioning of a school. Most organizations have levels of distinction, like "senior vice president," vice president," "executive director," and so on. In schools, very few teachers are merely instructing their students and performing the basic responsibilities of the classroom. This unidimensional outlook needs to go. Schools are small communities and serve students in tremendous ways outside of their learning needs.

Interestingly, in a company such as Amazon, you'll find various titles within one area. The "Fulfillment & Operations Managers [who] manage the heart of the Amazon shopping experience" hold several positions such as "Area Manager, Operations Manager, Flow Lead, Team Lead, Depot Manager, and Shift Manager" (Amazon, 2019).

Granted, schools are unlike Amazon in many ways, but the one parallel is the multifaceted dimensions within every role needed to operate the systems respectively. As educators, we can learn from industry in that each person's role does not need to be singular in nature, title, or description. Our departments can strategically delineate the different roles of each individual and the major purpose they play within a similar job.

Teachers do far more than teach, and when we lump all teachers into one big bucket, we don't recognize the uniqueness of what they do on the team, how they contribute to the success of the school, and the ways they go above and beyond the classroom. This is a critical first step in rewarding and retaining our talented teachers. In a practical sense, this might simply mean a title distinction but, whenever possible, it should mean extra pay for extra responsibilities, a stipend for the additional time and effort they put into the work, or the ability to use timesheets as a payment method for the additional hours they serve.

We certainly don't advocate that teachers should be paid for every hour above their required daily requirement; the job itself entails duties that go above most negotiated agreements, but we must begin to think "outside the box" of salaries alone when we make adjustments to how teachers might be rewarded for their contributions.

The second change is more technical and may require a slower timeline for implementation. We're advocating for fewer steps on the typical teacher salary scale. This means that new teachers start with a better salary in a system that doesn't necessarily reward teachers with pay for staying in the profession for longer periods of time, especially toward the end of their career. Consider a traditional pay scale that starts a new teacher at $36,000 annually and ends at $80,000 annually with five steps to go after year 25 of service. Suppose we create a smaller range, starting teachers at $60,000 and ending at $80,000, capping them at twenty-five years of service. This does mean that teachers won't get a step raise after twenty-five years, but it also means that they'll make far more money in their early years of teaching, and they'll benefit from regularly negotiated raises regardless.

Finally, we are advocating for a banded system of support and evaluation. Teachers who consistently demonstrate highly effective evaluations based on observations and clearly defined teaching competencies should be paid higher within a band. This means that each step in experience, say 1–5 years, also contains a band for "approaching," "effective," and "highly effective" to reward excellence in the classroom. We realize that this change comes with many implications, but doing what we've always done and expecting new results is not the answer either.

That's three distinct changes within the first shift; let's go deeper into the second shift as well.

The second shift in teacher career development must be based on improving teacher effectiveness throughout their career. On the one hand, we must invest in teachers as learners, not doers. The norm for professional development (PD) is that we are training teachers to do something new or different, which is often done in a large-group setting with the expectation that everyone will return the following day, ready to apply what they learned. But that's not how learning works. Recent findings suggest the need for an altogether different approach.

Buckingham and Goodall (2019) posit "that learning happens when we see how we might do something better by adding some new nuance or expansion to our own understanding. Learning rests on our grasp of what we're doing well" and then building on it. This requires leaders to help teachers identify patterns in effective teaching practices—within themselves, within others, and within the research—to uncover strengths and even glimpses of hope in areas that need to be developed more. This is why we're calling for micro-credentialing.

Micro-credentialing can be done in a very simple way at the school level all the way to the creation of complex structures tied to pay at the district and state levels. Nonetheless, learning should take a new turn for teachers so that they are building on their expertise over time, and it should be reflective of the needs of the school versus single-experience PD offerings that lead to very little transfer into the classroom. The key to micro-credentials is to place value in what it means for a teacher to become an expert at something related to classroom instruction.

A prime example is the Google Certified Educator program, but you can go beyond what outside organizations offer and develop internal mini-credentials at your school. Suppose you need your teachers to improve their use of collaborative structures for student engagement with the content. The traditional approach is to create *single* experiences in PLCs (professional learning communities), faculty meetings, and PD days. The credentialing approach requires a *series* of experiences to support learning over time along with indicators that substantiate that the teacher has mastered the use of the strategy. This means layering the professional learning and requiring mastery experiences for the earned credential.

When teachers have demonstrated that they understand and use the strategy with expertise, they are rewarded with the new credential.

Credentials can come with small rewards, as simple as prestige, title, and certificate. Or, they can reap greater rewards like traded time to use for make-up days (due to inclement weather), traded time to miss single-experience PD days, one-time monetary rewards, or even jumps in pay for specified periods of time.

The key is that professional learning experiences provide career development for teachers, honoring their expertise and building on their strengths. The results will yield greater teacher job satisfaction, retention, and better teaching and learning environments for students. Pay-for-performance systems are too often solely about student performance on single measures, which in some cases has led to illegal behavior among educators. This shift in teacher performance is to focus on how teachers are growing and engaging at work and ultimately improving their practice over time.

Couple these two shifts in career development with new notions of positive psychology—including what it means to be motivated, inspired, and energized at work—and you'll have well-developed, happy teachers who won't think twice about going to another school or another profession. Building a winning team of people who stick with your organization through "thick and thin" is critical to your ability to achieve success. Note that every angle or view of retention we've discussed so far comes from the perspective that people need a sense of support, satisfaction, and development.

"It turns out that relentless focus on people, on developing everyone in the organization, leads to an organizational culture designed for adaptive change" (Fleming, 2016). If we don't develop our teachers throughout their careers, our schools will never be agile enough to adapt to the technological advancements of the world or the ever-changing culture in which we live. Somehow schools exist as small microcosms of the past. The compulsory nature of school requires its users to adapt to it rather than the other way around. Add to that the almost nontransferable way in which we train teachers, treating them like buckets to fill rather than lifelong learners, and it's no wonder retention rates are at an all-time low.

Career development must be a top priority for the future of the profession and investing in people is the only way we're going to build the capacity of the workforce to combat burnout and drag. This also brings us to our three *Retention Accelerators*—motivation, inspiration, and energy.

GUIDING QUESTIONS

1. What are you currently doing to ensure that teachers are satisfied with their working conditions and fully engaged at work?
2. Does every teacher in your school feel that they have all of the resources needed to do their jobs well?
3. What opportunities does your school offer to teachers as career development experiences?

Chapter Two

Intrinsic Empowerment

My hope is that by understanding some of the hidden forces of motivation, we will find it easier to deploy the positive, intangible drivers that affect us all (Ariely, 2016, p. 102).

PRACTITIONER SPOTLIGHT: AMY FAST

When we spoke to Amy Fast, principal of McMinnville High School, about teacher motivation and retention, she hesitated, at first, to commit to any particular strategies that keep teachers happy at work. In fact, she said: "I struggle to illustrate the importance of empowering teachers in an anecdote because what I've found is that empowering and appreciating staff isn't about grand gestures or 'teacher appreciation week' but about showing up *for* them every single day and having our commitment to them and gratitude for them reflected in all the seemingly inconsequential day-to-day interactions."

Amy referenced Daniel Pink's (2009) *Drive*, and what it means to motivate, trust, and even protect our staff when it comes to inspiration at work. She raised thoughtful points about mandates and policies that prevent teachers from being "masters of their craft" with a "unique greatness" that leaders must unleash. She talked about empowerment from the standpoint of autonomy, mastery, and purpose.

The specifics of empowerment and motivation, the aspects of work that meaningfully engage staff and increase retention, are intangible. They are the feelings, emotions, and connections that permeate a culture. Genuine appreciation and support come from an intense care and authentic appreciation that we have for one another and the contributions that we each make to our work environment. Inspiration is organic and a manifestation of our attitude, outlook, and desire to achieve incredible results.

Amy did indicate a few key features of her school that create a culture that make it a great place for teachers to thrive. McMinnville High has a teacher-led podcast where a teacher leader interviews other staff members about their professional philosophies and classroom practices. The podcast gets posted on social media for the entire school community so that everyone can hear about the amazing work that might otherwise go unseen and untold.

For inspiration and appreciation, administrators write specific emails daily to staff, highlighting how their work is positively contributing to the school and the overall goals that they set. Finally, and of serious importance, Amy said, "we feed them frequently."

She spoke about the importance of breaking bread and the relationships formed in doing so. Nothing is more important than the "nourishment" that we get from a shared meal. You can learn more about what Amy Fast does to inspire students and staff by following her on Twitter @fastcrayon.

MOTIVATION AT WORK

Motivation in any area of our lives is very tricky. It's amazing how one day we can be filled with inspiration, focus, and energy, while another day we are fighting just to successfully manage our thoughts and time. Our fickle nature is nothing new and is interestingly highlighted by the timeless character of Ebenezer Scrooge in the classic *A Christmas Carol*. Dickens' novella is a beautiful account about the nature of people, the human condition, and what makes us tick. In a telling scene in which Scrooge is faced with his former business partner, the deceased Marley, he doesn't dismiss the existence of the ghost but he tells himself that the apparition isn't "real." He denies the authenticity of the image due to the simple reality that our senses, despite being designed to provide us with clarity, are easily deceived, any "little thing affects them. A slight disorder of the stomach makes them cheats" (Dickens, 1843, p. 19).

Being visited by an actual ghost in real life is a stretch, but Dickens reveals great insight into our human nature—our own surroundings, circumstances, events, and situations affect us on so many levels. At times, our own thoughts impact our ability to control our emotions, taking us into the past, present, and future of our minds. Our motivation seems to shift on a whim, exploited by our individual experiences and personal desires.

Acknowledging our natural human tendencies is paramount to motivating staff. It's possible that all of the greatest motivational leaders were first, either in the trade or within their hearts, some sort of cultural psychologists. Creating an environment designed to help employees realize their greatest strengths, connect deeply to their work, and achieve the desired results of the organization is only possible if you can tap into each person's mental state and personal sense of well-being.

At a glance, our individual core values don't naturally appear transferable to the organization's success. Because our motivation is often subject to our own senses, and our every effort can easily fall prey to any given sensation, leaders must prioritize motivation through purposeful and intrinsic means. Any other effort to motivate staff will be derailed or diminished by our human sensibilities.

To account for this, leaders must recognize that "the most powerful incentive known to humankind is our own evaluation of our behavior and accomplishments. When people are able to meet their personal standards, they feel validated and fulfilled" (Patterson, Grenny, Maxfield, McMillan, & Switzler, 2008, p. 94). Therefore, leaders who invest in their employees at the outset, from their hiring date and as an ongoing strategy throughout their careers, will effectively help them to understand their roles and what it means to be successful in the job.

This alone can lead to greater satisfaction, motivation, and retention. We must link each person's contribution to their ability to evaluate the importance of what they individually provide for the team. In other words, they need to see the work itself as an outcome and not necessarily some other long-range goal.

To create these conditions, we subscribe to the "law of the harvest," which asserts that we must focus on the process of our work, not just the outcome of it. The key feature of "the harvest" is to focus on the *giving* not the *getting*, the *sowing* not the *reaping* (Maxwell, 2012). It's especially true at work, but our natural mentality is to look for quick returns and daily tangible outcomes. Instead, in focusing on "sowing well," we prepare to wait for the harvest in due time. A good harvest is the result of meticulous planning, hard work, continual attention, good timing, and arguably a little luck. Farmers depend on and expect a successful harvest to survive—a belief that effort coupled with skill will yield commensurate results.

The benefit of the harvest is that its outcomes are clear, and often a laudable product results from the process undertaken and the effort expended. Administrators who sow well commit to the development of their employees and work toward intrinsic motivation, offering "enough support in the social context, so the natural, proactive tendencies are able to flourish" (Deci, 1996). Environments that naturally support and provide proactive structures, positive working conditions, and needed resources from day-to-day will generate long-term results. Most importantly, these environments create a stable staff that is committed to the organization because the organization is committed to them.

For a successful harvest, we must remember that development, motivation, and ultimately retention are forged within the working environment itself, centered on employees who know their purpose, who have a deep connection with the work and their colleagues, and who feel empowered as professionals. We call this *Intrinsic Empowerment*. Intrinsic empowerment comes from our ability to evaluate our successes as we sow, not just in what we reap. This is where an understanding of organizational psychology is critical for leaders. To motivate the people, we need to create a complete picture of their personal sensibilities so that they see their contributions on a regular basis.

The workers must gain enough perspective about their purpose to evaluate their contributions during the harvest rather than at the end of it. This type of visualization prompts intrinsic value in our daily efforts, giving us both a sense of efficacy and the hope needed to further engage in the process. It provides a vision for our success in solving the problems before us and results in both more effort toward the goals and happiness.

Considering the importance of the work facing education, these types of motivational and engaging environments are critical because they lead to greater success for students and staff. Let's examine the problem with lagging student performance on the math section of the state accountability measure or the SAT. Improving student math scores is not solved through the implementation of a program or a new curriculum. The results are also not seen on a regular basis through our daily work. This makes the goal seem unattainable and diminishes the daily work or, worse yet, distracts us from even doing it.

Better scores are a reality only when we commit to the hard work in uncovering the reasons why the scores are low—uncovering with precision the gaps that need to be filled to bring them up. Successful teams are motivated by the work at hand, not the outcomes. They don't let their minds wander into the future or beyond the relevant facts of the present situation. Any time a "ghost" appears, they quickly realize that it's merely an apparition and they pull themselves into focus, back to the sowing. At the center of any culture that can stay this focused is a leader who understands how purpose fulfillment works for *Intrinsic Empowerment*, so that she can be absent because others are able to refocus on their own.

Leaders who are completely tuned into creating meaning through the work at hand and their team's ability to evaluate their success in an ongoing way, not by some far-off goal or senseless quick fix, create cultures where people are fully engaged. They know that care must be taken in planting the seed for it to eventually grow and bear fruit. It's the meticulous gardening that delivers the finest rewards from any field.

In an environment of true motivation, the first of our *Retention Accelerators*, people will put forth every ounce of their effort because they feel connected to the work and celebrated for doing it. Their sense of intrinsic value provides license to keep pushing, even in the face of a phantom illusion or any made-up hindrance that haunts them.

Discretionary Effort

Nemours pediatric health system has ten powerful "Standards of Behavior" to govern its employees. Although each one is crucial and represents an aspect of the Nemours philosophy, the one that resonates with us in terms of motivation and retention is standard 3, "Volunteer

Discretionary Effort Constantly." One of the examples given states, "look for opportunities of improvement and make appropriate recommendations" (Nemours, 2009).

This expectation ties into *Intrinsic Empowerment* because it promotes an employee's discretion to recommend improvements any time they see an opportunity. Empowerment in improving the workplace and making recommendations is a problem-solving approach that not only motivates employees but creates happiness at work.

According to McKee (2018), "motivation that comes from inside us is a far more potent force than any carrot or stick used by our boss or the company" (p. 68). There's actually an additional psychological phenomena that goes with the potency of intrinsic motivation, which is the fact that people will become less motivated to do things that they like to do when it comes with an extrinsic reward (McKee, 2018).

In the world of education, this construct is something of considerable note because most educators are altruistic, coming to the field with an intrinsic notion of support and care for others. The minute these values are met with extrinsic reward to do more or get better is the minute that the reward actually counteracts any motivation to do the job at all. Too often leaders find themselves using a carrot-and-stick transactional leadership approach, but the only real way to motivate staff, especially in the public sector, is to work toward tapping into their discretionary effort.

Discretionary effort is defined by what we do to go above and beyond the requirements of our jobs, extending into the opportunities we see for making something better and using our effort, time, and energy to do more than is expected of us. Brandau and Ross (2018) define this kind of effort as what workers are *capable of* bringing to their tasks versus what they *have to do* to earn their pay. There's a huge gap between the amount of effort that employees can exert for the sake of the organization and the amount of effort it takes to get the job done. In schools, that gap makes up the difference between the ordinary and exceptional. A highly motivated staff means greater learning outcomes for students, positive working conditions, excitement, and fun.

To successfully build a culture where employees want to do more, leaders must invest in their people and abide by the laws of the harvest in doing so. The harvest analogy discussed above works to motivate staff in finding a purpose in the work at hand and not just the goals we set long range. In this case, discretionary effort comes from the same analogy in that we must learn to invest in people over time, planting seeds for their development without an immediate expectation that they change.

When supported and nurtured, employees exhibit discretionary effort because they know their work directly connects to the broader scope of the mission of the organization and the other divisions within the company, and they see how their work is impacting the greater community. As we invest in their growth, and they feel the impact of that investment within the organization, they give more of themselves. It becomes intrinsic motivation because of the feeling that employees get when they know their impact. Whether a healthcare system or a school, "perhaps the most transformational thing a company can do for its workforce is to invest in creating jobs and working environments that unleash intrinsic inspiration" (Garton, 2017).

The power of discretionary effort is that it's cyclical, benefiting the organization and the employee, creating a flywheel in the process. Employees who willingly go above and beyond each day positively impact the entire organization, not only through improved productivity but through creativity for innovation, through support for peers, and through synergy with new ideas. This "intense connection generates positive energy, and the more positive energy a person brings to work, the better he will do" (Hallowell, 2011, p. 75).

Seeing opportunity to serve in any possible way is a belief system that can be developed and recognized in any organization but is especially important in schools. When staff are recognized and heralded as an integral part of the school community, they are committed to the school and to the students, which means they won't consider leaving or searching for a better situation. Not only is discretionary effort a critical aspect of *Intrinsic Empowerment*, it supports retention and it defines the culture. It stems from a place of motivation, love, support, and, most of all, celebration for the work we do in schools.

Celebrations

Fueling the desire among employees to deliver results and give of themselves beyond their job requirements, establishing their own standards of excellence, is cultivated by the leader and delivered through the culture. Discretionary effort and celebratory cultures create intrinsic motivation for staff members to be their best and their happiest selves at work.

Genuine, authentic praise and acknowledgement that is intimately tied to the work being done each day motivates staff to do even more.

In fact, in organizations with high levels of discretionary effort and strong recognition, the leader is more concerned with too much effort and not enough balance than the other way around. Leaders who benefit from a highly motivated staff should always be looking for ways to cycle that energy back into the lives of the people who are giving their time, talents, and energy to the organization.

As Covey puts it, in *The Seven Habits of Highly Effective People* (1993), "always treat your employees exactly as you want them to treat your best customers" (p. 58). Just like your customers who keep coming back for more, so too will your employees when they feel valued and appreciated. The best thing about praising people and the work they do is that it's free. And, once this is ingrained within the culture as an organizational norm, similar to discretionary effort, it's actually quite easy to do. Despite its incredible benefits, though, we often fall short of delivering the level of praise necessary to change a school culture, improve morale, and reinforce the great work being done each day to achieve the established goals.

One reason that leaders fail to use recognition, celebrations, and praise is that "we're not fluent in the language of positive emotions in the workplace" (Schwartz, 2012). Leaders often know the facts regarding what praise can do for the team, but they don't know how to praise or celebrate effectively to lift the people and reap its benefits. The good news is that praising others is a skill that can be learned.

Another reason that leaders fail to recognize the accomplishments of others is due to so many myths regarding the problems that leaders face when they celebrate the team. Gostick and Elton (2007) list jealousy, inability to stay consistent, loss of meaning when done too often, and even the notion that we shouldn't lift people for doing what's expected of them. These myths are mere excuses, and if we care to truly engage our workforce, we must consider celebrating people as authentic tools to "strengthen [y]our work team" so that they can "achieve their full potential" (Gostick & Elton, 2007, p. 166).

To create a cultural shift that is built on recognition, celebrations must be an integral aspect in the fabric of the school, which means that it must be an active part of every meeting, event, and activity we have. Celebrating is a mindset that is geared to recognizing the smallest of wins and the largest of efforts (Thomas-EL, Jones, & Vari, 2020). Consistent appreciation reinforces the school's goals and recognizes achievements at every step of the way. As a result, incremental gains are valued, success is rewarded, and accomplishments are shared among everyone. The pursuit of achievement is a long road that is filled with many highs and lows. Celebrations are no different than well-planned watering stations during any 5K foot race. They are strategically placed throughout the course to provide needed hydration at critical junctures to support the runners who are giving it their all.

Celebrations reinforce the team's path by demonstrating a mile marker met, and they build teams by specifically praising what the team is striving to achieve. "The simple but transformative act of a leader expressing appreciation to a person in a meaningful and memorable way is the missing accelerator that can do so much and yet is used so sparingly" (Gostick & Elton, 2007, p. 8–9). Praise and celebration are not always natural to every leader, but like any other important skill, they are essential to practice. Because praise and celebration are necessary for support and motivation, leaders must become skillful at both.

Celebration is the consistent nourishment needed throughout the harvest for the results to be plentiful. From the planting to the growing, recognizing others fuels their desire to keep pushing and can intrinsically inspire the team to work hard and put forth their every effort. Specific praise is a constant reminder of the big picture, the purpose for the work, and it keeps the team motivated even when the goals seem long-off or insurmountable. The following technical tip offers a way to formulate praise so that it works to achieve its intended goal. Because praising people is a leadership skill, it can be broken down as a technique and practiced for mastery.

TECHNICAL TIP: PRAISE PRACTICE—A MODEL FOR SPECIFIC PRAISE

"When we receive expressions of gratitude, my research shows, we are more likely to persist when the road gets tough" (Gino, 2018, p. 173). Providing praise is critical because it not only prompts pride in the work and the desire to repeat a behavior, it motivates us to keep working hard. Too often, though, even when leaders provide what they believe is praise, the praise itself fails to make a difference for two primary reasons: 1) Leaders feel like they're delivering praise, but workers don't recognize the comments (written or verbal) as being praise, and 2) The praise is so ambiguous that the workers have no idea why they are being praised in the first place. This means that employees simply don't feel as if their work is valued, which is the primary element in motivation.

In this "Technical Tip," we provide a model for specific praise so that using praise can be replicable and explicit. If leaders struggle to find the right words and phrases, then the work lies in deliberate practice using very direct language that is undeniably the leader's celebration of the employee's work.

Let's use instructional feedback as an example. There are any number of reasons to praise the work of teachers, but leaders often find themselves striving to improve instructional practices. This is a place where praise can work perfectly to motivate. The conundrum is that it will motivate when done well and demotivate when done poorly.

As we make our way into classrooms, we want to support the strategies that work best for student learning. This means that we want to praise teachers for using pedagogical approaches that are both research- and evidence-based. We know that approximately 95 percent of what teachers choose to do with students on any given day will work with an effect size of between .20 and .40 (Hattie, 2009). As instructional leaders, we're looking for strategies that leverage the highest effects on learning. And while average effect sizes hover around .40, there are numerous strategies that have effect sizes that double the average.

But we're not talking about instructional practices here as much as we're learning to use a technical tip, specific praise, as a motivator. That said, motivation is directional, and we want to face the teacher in the right direction as we motivate her to push forward. Specific praise is the motivational technique.

In the use of praise for instructional practices, it's used when we see teachers doing something very specific that we want the teacher to be *proud* of doing and to *repeat* in subsequent scenarios. Praise is used for *pride in the work* and *replication of the practice*. Finally, in our model of praise, we advocate that specific praise should be kept for use in only scenarios were we see either effort or excellence (what we call E^2)—and nothing else. This means that teachers are either praised for working hard (as in trying something new) *or* for excelling in an area of focus.

The magic in this type of praise is specificity—the teacher knows for certain what is being recognized because of the choice language that specifies the observer's delight. Because leaders need to be focused on these two areas—specificity and appreciation—our format helps them with what we call *Praise Practice*. Let's take a look. Specific praise has a unique format that can be used in a number of ways, but these two formats work well in the development phase of learning to provide praise more often:

1. Make a praise statement, be specific about what you're praising, provide a rationale for the praise, make a praise statement.
2. Be specific about what you're praising, make a praise statement, provide a rationale for the praise, make a praise statement.

Notice that it's a four-part model, and although the parts are interchangeable, it's critical to use specific praise statements twice to anchor what is being recognized. Let's take a look at two samples of an administrator praising a teacher:

1. Mrs. Jones, I really like your planned collaborative structures today. The specificity of the partnering strategy ensured accountability for all students. Students benefit from that level of direction for peer-to-peer interactions because it supports retention and quality collaboration and communication. You did an awesome job with the lesson today.
2. Mrs. Jones, your students were really working together within your planned collaborative structures today; the directions were crystal clear. It was impressive. We've been focused on cooperative learning, and it's critical that our learners are supported with structures like this one. It was a model activity that reflects the level of excellence that we are looking for in our classrooms.

In the praise statements above, you'll notice how the four-part model is used and how we doubled-down on the praise statements. You might emphasize what you're praising or the rationale, either one works well, but be sure to use two praise statements to avoid ambiguity and to truly recognize the great work being done. A teacher should feel recognized and valued after reading your praise.

Always remember that we cannot give enough genuine specific praise. For any given lesson, you might provide three pieces of specific praise during one classroom visit, which supports the teacher and reinforces what they are doing with at least six praise statements. The more praise you give, using specific examples of what works within the lesson, the greater the chance that the teacher will duplicate those practices in upcoming lessons. Praise becomes the fulcrum for consistently excellent classroom practices.

As leaders, we should always consider two questions regarding the language we use when giving feedback:

1. What do I want the teacher *to think or feel* based on the feedback?
2. What do I want the teacher *to do* based on the feedback?

The answer when using specific praise should always be the same: 1) I want the teacher to feel proud and affirmed in her work, and 2) I want her to repeat this behavior again. Let's examine a simple scenario.

Scenario:

Mrs. Greenwald is a third-year teacher in your school, and she's always open to feedback about her lessons. It's not uncommon for her to quickly check her computer as soon as you leave the room after a walkthrough so that she can read your comments right away.

Today, her students are in "centers." There are five centers total with six students at each one. The students are working in groups of three so she has two groups at each center. You walk over to the first center and the kids are ready and eager to share what they're thinking and doing.

Students are collecting evidence from different reading passages. The first part of the center experience is a silent read of the article/passage, then students have roles for evidence collection onto a graphic organizer, and they work together to gather all the information they need. Mrs. Greenwald supports students by circulating the room, and she spends a good amount of time at each group. She's asking high-level questions to prompt thinking.

You stay long enough for her to transition students to the next activity. The passages are short so they only have 12 minutes at each table. It's great to see this amount of reading, summarizing, and collaboration in a science classroom. You ask the students what they'll do with the information, and they say it's an individual essay with a group presentation. You hit send and move to your next walkthrough.

Sample Feedback with Specific Praise:

> Mrs. Greenwald,
>
> I really liked the energy in your room today as I entered. Students were up and moving around in a controlled manner, timed by you, and making their way to the centers to collect evidence from the reading passages you planned for them. Student movement is supported by brain research, and it's critical for our learners to move around. Very well planned. Thank you.
>
> I also liked how they read quietly for a short time, and then talked about the reading. It's so important that they have quiet time coupled with think- and talk-time. Be proud of the way that transpired.
>
> I really appreciate the collaborative structure you used with the groups of three. It was thoughtful of you, and I could tell that they all had specific roles. The students could explain the focus for the day and that the end-goal is an individual essay along with a group presentation. The rigor with the essay is on grade level, and you continue to support communication and oracy with the presentation outcome. I am thoroughly pleased with what I saw.
>
> Finally, your support for the school literacy initiative is evident and clear. You have students reading with specific time spent on short passages, summarizing text, and synthesizing evidence from multiple passages. I commend these efforts, and I'm excited to read an essay or two when the students are finished. Fantastic visit.
>
> —Mr. Hoover

Note that Mr. Hoover was able to provide four pieces of specific praise using the four-point model.

Activity:

Independently, or with your team, identify the four parts of the model in each of the four paragraphs, noting where the feedback uses praise statements, specific actions, a rationale for the feedback, and a second praise statement. Note also how this type of feedback is likely to make Mrs. Greenwald *feel* and how she may *respond* in return.

GUIDING QUESTIONS

1. How can you further develop each staff member's discretionary effort and intrinsic empowerment for the betterment of your school culture?
2. Are your celebrations uplifting, motivational, and fun, or do they need a boost to improve staff morale?
3. What steps do you need to take to provide specific praise more often, using the model provided in the Technical Tip?

Chapter Three

Dealing with the Depths of Despair

The human desire to identify and spark a purposeful light in our days is a very real part of our orientation to work—where after all, we spend most of our waking hours (Hedges, 2017, p. 177).

PRACTITIONER SPOTLIGHT: BASIL MARIN

We connected with Basil Marin about the value of inspiration in schools. If you know Basil, or you've heard his message, you know that he's an inspirational person who harnesses his full potential. He was clear when he told us, though, that it's not enough for one person, even the leader, to provide or be the only source of inspiration in schools. In fact, what he talked about was reciprocity. When we discussed school leadership and teacher retention, he described a cycle of inspiration whereby the inspired are responsible to celebrate others and foster a culture of encouragement so that inspiration is contagious.

Basil described the transformation of a school where he worked earlier in his career. He called it a "mindset shift." The school started a social and emotional learning initiative, and Basil assigned teachers as "advocates" for students who were struggling. At first, the teachers were skeptical, questioning how they would fit "one more thing" into the curriculum or find any time to meet with students outside of their classes.

But Basil believed deeply in the advocacy program and continually reinforced the mantra that "students don't care how much you know until they know how much you care." The ones who weren't learning were also the ones without a connection with an adult at school.

Building trusting relationships is difficult. We often take for granted that classrooms are spaces where friendships are easily shared, where the bond between students and teachers is natural. But that's not always the case. The challenge is that teachers must build relationships and teach. Covering the content of the course and giving assessments is not a natural relationship builder, especially when students struggle in school. The goal is for teachers to build strong relationships through their instructional prowess. Meaningful engagement, connectivity, and relevance are some of the hallmark traits of these master teachers.

Unfortunately, some teachers are great at relationships, but have limits to their pedagogy, while others are content experts, but don't build strong relationships easily. This isn't a knock on educators but an admission that effective teachers possess both skills and use them masterfully. Great administrators acknowledge this dichotomy in skills and face them head-on. Basil learned quickly that he needed to coach and support the teachers in their efforts to build relationships with students just as much as he needed to lead instruction.

Soon enough, the success stories emerged and provided evidence that the culture was shifting. Little by little, attitudes of both students and teachers evolved and changed. As student advocates, teachers who had strong relationships with certain students gave tips and guidance to other teachers who needed to make a connection. Discipline referrals plummeted and inspiration swelled. Each time a teacher would tell a story about a breakthrough, it fueled others to try new strategies and work even harder at making deeper connections.

The powerful aspect of this exchange is that the teachers inspired one another to make greater investments in the lives of the students. This sparked joy, determination, and achievement. With Basil's courage to take the first steps in tackling a complex school culture need, a change occurred in the hearts and minds of the community. That's precisely what defines an inspired, happy, and purpose-driven group of educators.

A key indicator of strong leadership is when initiatives remain even after the person who brought them to life has left the organization. Basil returned to the school for a visit, after taking a position in a different state, to find the culture of advocacy still going strong. Teachers explained that the mentoring remained constant and that every inspirational transformation that was made only fueled the teachers to work harder to transform the school one student at the time.

He told us that "many of the young men who were wreaking havoc on the school when I got there are now leaders." The school changed because the people adopted a "mindshift" and embraced a new way of supporting one another. That's inspiration at work. You can learn more about school leadership and inspiration from Basil Marin by following him on Twitter @basil_marin.

INSPIRATION AT WORK

"Creating inspiration—whether through leaders or through investment in the employees themselves—is now essential for attraction and retention of the best talent" (Horwitch & Whipple, 2014). An inspired workforce is critical in the creation of a positive culture in schools, and great leaders work to inspire their employees for the betterment of everyone and the organization. Whether the goal is to retain teachers through the creation of an inspirational school environment or because inspired workers exert greater effort, the result is a happier staff with a deeper sense of purpose at work.

The truth is that it takes "two-and-a-quarter satisfied employees to generate the same output as one inspired employee" (Garton & Mankins, 2015). This makes the creation of inspirational work environments a moral imperative of school leaders. Not only do we owe it to our staff, we owe it to the students and the communities from which they come. When teachers are inspired, they work harder through joy and determination, and they are far more likely to stay on the team for the long run.

"The good news is that inspirational leadership can be taught, and it can be learned" (Garton & Mankins, 2015). But this good news also comes with a touch of despair, which is that most people in supervisory positions weren't likely taught how to be inspirational leaders at work. There are two reasons for this: 1) Most leadership development programs "leave inspiration skills off the list" of competencies, and 2) "Training for inspirational skills involves much more than conventional leadership development programs [especially school leadership development programs] can offer" (Horwitch & Whipple, 2014).

That said, you didn't make it this far into a leadership development book, one that claims to help you inspire your school culture, to be told that the work is impossible or that you lack a skill that we can't help you to cultivate. There are, in fact, very specific ways in which you can deepen your leadership dexterity by becoming more inspirational for your staff. We offer a "Four Cs" model for becoming an inspirational leader. You can inspire others in many ways but start with these four Cs to improve your ability to inspire the people you lead at work. For each of the Cs, we note some of our favorite resources as a place to start.

Four Cs Model for Inspirational Leadership

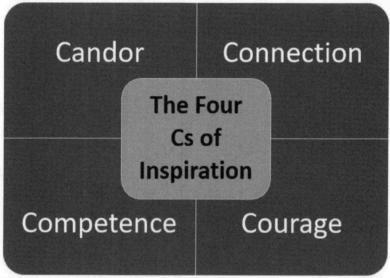

Figure 3.1.   The Four Cs of Inspiration. Image created by author.

First, a primary way that we inspire at work is by galvanizing the trust that we have on the team. Interestingly, though, is that developing trust can be counterintuitive. We have to be careful to make sure that we don't associate trust with something that stems from good will and tolerance. This type of thinking fails to build the type of trust needed for organizational and individual improvement because our generosity and kindheartedness can trap us in a "circle of nice," keeping us from saying what is truly on our minds with regard to the culture and the effectiveness of our practices (Jones & Vari, 2019). Covey (2006) brings to light several of these types of contradictions about establishing trust in much of his work on the subject. Although we might think that it's about being "nice" to others, instead it requires us to use "talk straight" to "confront reality" and to "clarify expectations." That's why our first C of inspiration is *Candor*. Candor is the driving force for clarity, and it also allows us to demonstrate compassion for people through sincerity and open dialogue (Jones & Vari, 2019). Leaders who use candor move faster, solve problems more quickly, unleash others to do meaningful work, and build strong relationships. You can start to inspire others today through the use of candid conversations, and if you're not comfortable with embarking on this approach to leading right away, but you do want to be more inspirational for your team, instead of working on inspiration itself, set out to learn more about candid conversations as a first step on your journey.

You can read *Candid and Compassionate Feedback: Transforming Everyday Practice in Schools* (Jones & Vari, 2019), which is about using candor to improve best practices in schools, or you can pick up a more business-driven book that we recommend called *Radical Candor: Be a Kick-Ass Boss Without Losing Your Humanity* by Kim Scott (2017). These are just two examples of places where you can start to learn to be more candid as the first aspect of creating an inspirational workplace.

This brings us to our next C in the model, which is *Connection*. To retain people in any organization, they must feel a deep connection to their tasks and to the other people with whom they work. The team has to connect to both the mission and to one another. You can learn to be more inspirational by simply interacting more with others. "Developing an inspirational ability requires the motivation to increase self-awareness, embrace new ways of interacting, reflect upon their impact and revise your approach" (Horwitch & Whipple, 2014). This means that you need to find ways to make deeper connections with your team, including telling your personal story and allowing others to do the same.

We tend to think that "business is not personal," but that's not true. Great teams take the work to heart in a very personal way, and they connect through the power of storytelling. And, it starts with leaders who captivate as they share:

From their individual set of traumas, experiences, longings, failures, triumphs, and histories, they have a unique way of looking at the world, and they share their special vision through powerful stories that pluck at our heartstrings and stimulate our thinking and our emotions in ways that literally no one else can. (Caprino, 2012)

The most powerful way that we make connections with others is by telling our stories to one another. Leaders can be guarded, especially when they feel the weight of the world on their shoulders, but your team needs to know that you are a real person with real feelings. When we make deep connections through personal stories, we bring our authentic selves to the work, and that creates strong teams with greater inspiration and stronger retention.

But don't fret if you're an introvert who agonizes over telling your personal account of an experience to groups of people. There are books to read and seminars that can help. *The Story Skills Workshop* is one place to go. Led by Bernadette Jiwa and Seth Godin, it provides a frame-work, step-by-step process, and even the courage to tell your story.

The third C in our inspiration model is *Courage*. Inspirational leaders create positive cultures by being brave and encouraging others to do the same. If you want your team to go out on a ledge, to think differently, or to take risks in becoming great, you need to demonstrate how that should be done and that it's safe to do so. We tend to think that great managers are versatile with the ability to take on any role as needed, but that's not true. "They must be spiky, not well-rounded . . . and provide the key players the freedom they need to continue to excel" (Garton, 2017). Inspirational leaders put others first, helping them to overcome "deep challenges" (Caprino, 2012). They have the courage to get out of the way, and they don't manage others directly with the way that they would do the work. They hire people with unique talents and then they support their new ideas and challenges to the current system.

This takes bravery and a rebellious spirit, but it's exactly how we inspire others to take action against the status quo (Gino, 2018). Hess (2013) calls this type of inspiring school leader a "cage-buster." Cage-busters work to solve problems that others consider to be insurmount-able, and through their courage, they inspire others to "think ambi-tiously about how to create great schools and . . . what it takes to make them real" (Hess, 2013, p. 6).

You can inspire your team by taking risks and, as you do, your following will become stronger and even more loyal to the way that you create a path for success. Supposing you need some inspiration to be a risk-taker at work, we recommend the work of Brené Brown, *Dare to Lead: Brave Work. Tough Conversations. Whole Hearts* (2018) and Kimberly Davis, *Brave Leadership: Unleash Your Most Confident, Powerful, and Authentic Self to Get the Results You Need* (2018).

Our fourth and final C is *Competence*. Leaders must be able to use their vision and strengths to support the team and continue to grow in their ability to add value to the organization. "Too often managers underestimate how much time and effort it takes to keep growing and developing" (Hill & Lineback, 2011). We've seen it time and time again where leaders become so focused on growing the team that they fail to take opportunities to grow themselves. Competent, effective leaders are not skillful because they gained proficiency in an area of management and then maintained that same level of skill throughout their careers. Instead, they find areas of strength about themselves and then concentrate on developing those skills. As Ray Kroc asked, "are you green and growing or ripe and rotting?"

Additionally, inspirational leaders do not work to be excellent in every aspect of leading. "An individual can multiply his inspirational leadership ability by excelling at just a handful of distinguishing strengths and neutralizing his weakness, rather than trying to be exceptional at everything" (Horwitch & Whipple, 2014). Leaders inspire others by lifting them into positions of power and influence, especially into positions and areas that the leader sees as his own deficit. Great leaders surround themselves with greatness. Rather than trying to excel past the people they lead, they develop competence in themselves in a few specific areas and then fill the gaps with everyone else on the team.

Two books that support your growth for both confidence in yourself and others as well as becoming competent by surrounding yourself with great people are *Make Yourself Unforgettable* (2011) by the Dale Carnegie Training team and *Permission to Screw Up* (2017) by Kristen Hadeed. These two resources will help you to see what competence is all about, and it's not always about your personal skills in any area of the organization.

One throughline in our inspiration model is the need to unleash and empower people. Each of our Cs have a dimension that requires the leader to let go by granting others the power and authority to make decisions for the betterment of the team. Through candor, connection, courage, and competence, great leaders entrust others with the work at hand. Collins (2001) tells readers that the minute you *feel* the need to micromanage, you've made a critical hiring mistake, which is why it's vital that you understand the reasons why you *feel* this way about providing the additional oversight.

The feeling could be because you, in fact, made a mistake in hiring the wrong person. Maybe they don't have the right skills, or they're simply not a good fit within the culture. But your "feeling" may not be a hiring mistake at all. Sometimes it's not a hiring mistake that's causing your need to closely supervise; instead, it's a flaw in your leadership.

Micromanagement can mask itself in our minds as a response to the poor performance of an employee; yet, in reality, it's a response that some leaders have when they feel disconnected to the ranks or when they become insecure that the team won't achieve its desired results (Knight, 2015). This is not an employee issue but rather a leadership issue. Problematic in many ways, micromanagement produces drastically negative results for retention, cited as "the fastest way to push top talent out the door" (DesMarais, 2016). Simply put, micromanagement is the opposite of inspiration at work, and practicing to be inspirational using our 4Cs model will help you to stop micromanaging in your school or district.

It's critical, though, that as you practice the 4Cs, you also reflect on the basic premise of the model, which is to inspire others through empowerment. Candid, connected, courageous, and competent leaders are the ones that relinquish the most control as they build teams that are inspired to achieve greatness.

Finally, there are two other areas of inspiration that we want to touch upon. First, it's of growing importance for leaders to recognize what positive psychologists are revealing regarding *happiness* at work. In the next section, we dive into employee happiness as an outcome of a great working environment. Second, a major contributor to inspiration is having a clear *purpose* in the workplace. Being purposeful about purpose is a key aspect to leading better and helping others to have a vision for themselves from day to day. Happiness and purpose are not merely social constructs but rather are defined in the ways that leaders model and implement them in schools and districts.

Happiness

Workplace happiness is the result of a leader who cares about the joyfulness of a positive working environment and the productivity that ensues when everyone is cheerful. The outcome is a lively group of well-intentioned, good-spirited people who care about one another and the important responsibilities they have on the team. School leaders have an obligation to focus on happiness, and there are several ways to make it a priority. We want to target two ways that are effective and can be put into practice right away—generosity and social investments. Together they create what we call *Habitual Happiness Highpoints* (H3). H3s are consistent ways in which we elevate our attitudes by giving to the community and showing care for one another.

First, *generosity* is a key component to feeling happy in life and work (Kelada, 2018). Generous schools, those that create service experiences for students and staff, are always happier places to work. You can increase the *Habitual Happiness Highpoints* (H3) for your staff by ensuring that you consistently promote and support the ways in which your school can give back to the community. And this doesn't have to be driven by fundraisers and asking people for money. There are many ways to create what we call a *Giving School*. *Giving Schools* are community-based schools that have regular and seamless ways in which students and staff integrate with the community to show gratitude through service-based learning.

You can start by making a list of monthly activities that you can celebrate through acts of generosity. When your school contributes philanthropically, and you celebrate your achievements, it makes for a happier place to work. Commit to a once-a-month schedule of local events for staff and students to attend as volunteers. Assemble a team of students and staff to oversee both the contributions as well as the celebrations of their commitment to giving back. Your monthly faculty meeting is a great place to highlight each of the success stories. When we consistently demonstrate the power in our *H3 Giving School* culture, people are simply happier at work.

Second, Achor (2010) reveals that happiness is a byproduct of our *social investment*. "In the midst of challenges and stress, some people choose to hunker down and retreat within themselves" (Achor, 2010, p. 18). But that only creates silos of loneliness and despair. Because schools can be places with daily stressors, we need social investments in each other to build safeguards against negative thoughts and burnout. Make a list of monthly activities whereby the staff can be social with one another. This isn't just about bowling after work but rather the ways in which we engage socially before, during, and after school. "When you have a manager who cares about your happiness and your success, your career and your life, you end up with a better job, and it's hard to imagine working anywhere else" (Goler, Gale, Harrington, & Grant, 2018).

Social investments are frequent lifts that we make for one another, as simple as "shoutouts" during announcements and as elaborate as Beth Houf's Room Service Cart (find it on Twitter @BethHouf). The point is that we devote ourselves to making the workplace as fun as possible. *H3 Giving Schools* include both philanthropic endeavors for staff and students to give back in the community, which promotes *generosity*, and they make *social investments* within the organization. Both generosity and social investments intentionally create *Habitual Happiness Highpoints* for the team. It's through giving and social togetherness that we find purpose in the workplace.

One final point about happiness at work, Coyle, in *The Culture Code* (2018), reveals that "one misconception about highly successful cultures is that they are happy, lighthearted places. This is mostly not the case. They are energized and engaged, but at their core their members are oriented less around achieving happiness than around solving problems together" (p. 55). The key is that the energy and engagement through problem-solving is what makes these cultures happy places to work. The culture looks "happy" and "lighthearted" because of the connection that the people are making to the work and to one another. Happiness is not the goal in doing the work, necessarily, but it is a byproduct of the work itself. The focus is not on making people happy but rather on happiness as the outcome of generous, purposeful work.

Generosity + Social Investments = H3 Giving Schools

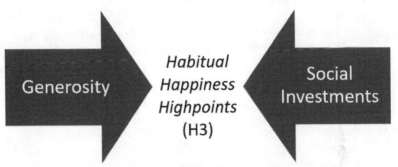

Figure 3.2.   Habitual Happiness Highpoints. Image created by author.

Purpose

"We give more of ourselves when we have an impact—even if it's a small one" (McKee, 2018). For a staff to experience the highest degrees of inspiration and the greatest sense of connection to the work, they need constant reminders of their purpose and impact. Although schools play such an important role in the sustainability of our communities, including economic development and healthy living conditions, the schools themselves don't innately grasp the fruits of their labor. In other words, because students are often long gone by the time our impact is realized, living the lives that their schools helped them to create, educators don't clearly see their influence on a day-to-day basis.

Of course, we all revel in the visit from a former student who tells us about the positive changes that we made on her life, but that's not a daily norm. For this reason, school leaders need strategies for reminding all staff of their purpose and significance by building structures to identify the impact that is being made by the team.

We promote three intentional ways that leaders can help teachers and other staff to bring their purpose to the forefront as often as possible. We call this the *Professional Purpose Process* (PPP). Monthly staff meetings are a great place where purpose can be solidified and expressed.

1. The first layer of the PPP is for the staff to create and communicate their own *Personal Work Purpose* (PWP). We modified this reflection activity from Tate's (2017) *The Purpose Project*. It's a simple reflection activity where staff can write a one-sentence PWP to galvanize the significance of what they do. This can become a staple during staff meetings where people review, revise, and share their purpose and accomplishments. Plus, it's fun.

2. The second layer of the PPP is to include a *Daily Purpose Reminder* (DPR) in your communication with staff. This can happen in every conversation, meeting, announcement, walkthrough, etc. Any time we're communicating with staff, they need a DPR to emphasize the *why* behind our actions. You can use both the PWP and the school's vision to remind people of their collective or individual purpose, but the key is to be consistent.

3. The last layer of the PPP is a *Purpose Commitment Coin* (PCC). Leaders can carry PCCs and give them to employees who are clearly making a difference. PCCs can be rare, given only a few times a year, or they can be distributed daily, collected by staff for prizes and rewards of some sort. The point is that leaders who care about motivation, create ways to clarify purpose. The tangible aspect of the coin gives it life long after it's shared.

Through your PPP, you can communicate purpose using PWPs, DPRs, and PCCs. These efforts are often overlooked and underused because they seem awkward or forced, but the power in using them is that they remind us about what we are striving to achieve each day. It's easy to lose focus and fall into a rut, which is what the PPP works to prevent. For any of these strategies to make a difference, they require commitment and energy from the leader. The truth is that once you invest in your staff this way, it will fuel their inspiration and energize you right back.

Personal Work Purpose + Daily Purpose Reminder +
Purpose Commitment Coins = Professional Purpose Process

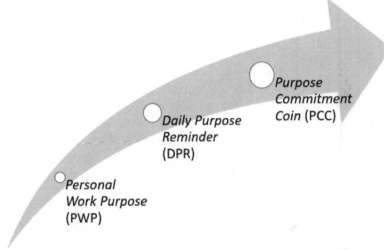

Figure 3.3. Professional Purpose Process. Image created by author.

TECHNICAL TIP:
DOGS AND LIZARDS AND MONKEYS, OH, MY!

Let's take a quick look into the ruts and ruins of life without a meaningful workplace, where happiness and purpose are void. We don't have far to go before we'll find the depths of despair. Over two-thirds of the workforce is disengaged, which is why Mechlinski (2018) calls for a time when our work is connected with our passion, using not only our minds but also our guts and hearts to guide us. And there are ways to overcome the humdrum, for yourself and others, but they take mental agility and the self-awareness to realize when you need to make the shift in your day or life. It's the mental game that can drive us mad or keep us going. We offer three tips from three of our favorite authors.

First, author Jon Gordon, in his book, *The Positive Dog*, tells readers that we have two dogs within us, a positive dog and a negative dog (2012). The key to happiness, according to the fable, is to simply feed the positive dog. "The more we feed the positive dog the bigger it gets and the stronger it becomes" (Gordon, 2012, p. 87). The positive dog is able to overcome the negative dog but only when you feed one over the other. As humans, we have the opportunity to provide nourishment for our negative thoughts by allowing them to exist, feeding them with more negativity. Or we can feed our own positive thoughts, growing stronger over time as positive people.

"The research shows that we can develop more positivity in our lives and share it with those around us, at work and at home" (Gordon, 2012, p. 87). Gordon (2012) offers an eleven-part plan: among his suggestions, he includes a celebration of a daily success, spending time with positive people, and coaching others. The point is that positivity begets positivity. The more you celebrate, surround yourself with other uplifting people, and help others to see the goodness in the world, the more you'll grow your positive muscles to be able to do so even in the toughest of times. We challenge you to read *The Positive Dog* and take the "Positive Pledge" (Gordon, 2012, p. 97).

Second, speaker and author, Seth Godin, discusses the critical theory of the lizard brain. In *Linchpin* (2010), Godin says that our lizard brains "will invent stories, illnesses, emergencies, and distractions in order to keep the genius bottled up." It's loud and afraid, and its purpose is to squash your ability to be rational. It's millions of years old, associated with the flight-or-fight process in our neocortex. It's job is to scare you into thinking that you're in danger. This means that instead of thriving on change, positivity, and forward momentum, the oldest part of our brains will actually activate a response to hold on to the status quo, even if it's what's causing our misery.

To overcome the forces of nature that are baked into our lizard brains since the early days of our existence, we must first be self-aware. It's only when we're cognizant of our lizard brain that we can push past the emotional resistance that we have toward change. Noticing that our gut response is to hold on to old practices, even when they don't produce results, is the first step in the process of liberation. Humans often find discord in trying something new, but we also experience dissonance with our current circumstances.

We don't like change, and we don't like the way things are. To disrupt the cycle, we must realize when our lizard brains are telling us to accept the status quo and respond by forcing our own minds to focus on the purpose of our work, not our negative feelings about it. The irony is that in doing so, we can become happier and even more inspired to explore new things more often in the future.

Third, Todd Whitaker, well-known school leadership guru, says that "misguided leadership can damage a workplace, alienate customers, and otherwise make life annoying, even miserable, for lots of people" (2014, p. 1). According to Whitaker (2014), life at work is swarming with monkeys. These are not the cute and cuddly monkeys you may be imagining. The monkeys he refers to are burdens, lurking around corners and hanging on the backs of anyone who can't handle their negative imposition.

Too often, though, as we "shift the monkey" from one person's back to another, we appease the problem-maker by relocating the difficulty versus transferring the weight back onto the monkey herself. Because of this, "negative, poorly performing people tend to get a disproportionate amount of power, attention, and empathy. They continue to behave obnoxiously and unfairly because they're rewarded for doing so" (Whitaker, 2014, p. 4).

To get rid of loud, unproductive people, we shift their complaints away from them, burdening our schools so that we can lighten the load of the monkey's impact. But the opposite occurs. Instead, we should always shift the load back onto the monkey so that her strain is not placed on the team but rather becomes the sole responsibility of the monkey herself. Whitaker offers two important antidotes, among other suggestions, which are to always make decisions based on the best people in the organization and to protect the highest performers first and foremost. We need to be intentional about shifting the monkeys away from the people we want to retain, motivate, inspire, and energize, and force the negative people to shoulder their own troubles, complaints, worries, and blame.

Whether it's your negative dog, lizard brain, or workplace monkey, for people to be inspired and happy at work, they need to find their purpose and recognize the forces of evil that can pull us into the depths of despair. To retain top talent, leaders need to understand the pressures and persuasions of natural and environmental origin. The culture of a school can be one that provides inspiration or it can be one that sucks it dry. Unleashing and empowering people takes candor, connection, courage, and competence, but we must always be sure that we're using the 4Cs with the right mindset and with the right people.

GUIDING QUESTIONS

1. How are you deliberately working on your ability to communicate with candor, your connections with people, your courage as a leader, and your strengths within the organization?
2. How can your school become an *H3 Giving School* through acts of generosity within the community and social investments in the people who work there?
3. Which aspects of the *Professional Purpose Process* can you employ in your position to keep people from feeding their negative dogs, thinking with their lizard brains, or accepting the grief from the workplace monkeys?

Chapter Four

Talent + Enthusiasm

As energy and mental resilience increase, we experience vigor. Bring together dedication, absorption, and vigor, and employees are highly engaged (Gino, 2018, p. 173).

PRACTITIONER SPOTLIGHT: JESSICA GRANT

Jessica Grant reached out to share a powerful and inspirational experience. As a new assistant principal at Northview Elementary School, she understood the importance of adjusting quickly in her new school, but what eclipsed her concern for herself was eight new teachers. Suddenly their needs were paramount and how well they were acclimating to their new situation became the first priority.

Despite frequent visits and regularly observing the teachers, she quickly recognized that the feedback conversations weren't enough support. She thought to herself: "What else can I do? Teacher burnout is real. We have to do something for our teachers so that they can take care of our students." This is a common thought, but the actual support that came next is the real challenge. Fortunately, Jessica acted on her intuition.

It was September, as she recalled, and not knowing exactly what steps to take, she decided to go directly to the source. To set appropriate goals, to meet the new teachers where they were, and to respond with her best effort, she developed a survey for the new hires. As Jessica reviewed the data, the results were clear. Luckily, she knew right away how she could provide assistance.

The new teachers wanted two things: 1) They wanted professional learning experiences on the specific topic of classroom management, and 2) They wanted more support from seasoned staff and administrators. "These new teachers needed mentors," she told us. And so she developed what she called the New Teacher Academy, a fully integrated mentoring program with coaching support, professional learning opportunities, and a network of experienced teachers who willingly participated.

The New Teacher Academy incorporated multiple layers of support, including monthly sessions "where novice teachers and mentors would engage in discussions around a special classroom topic or strategy." The mentors and mentees were deliberately paired with specifically identified days for the mentors to model instructional practices for the new hires. At the end of the year, Jessica polled the group again, and the results were not surprising. Jessica said that it "solidified the program" for the future. All of the teachers were grateful for the experience, they felt supported, and, best yet, even the mentors were energized by the work.

Jessica told us that she also realized how the academy benefited everyone involved. All educators need support throughout their career to develop and grow, but learning isn't always the result of *receiving*, it also comes from *giving*. New teachers benefit immensely from having a mentor; experienced teachers benefit from being one, and as a result, the school community thrives— a true win-win. You can learn more from Jessica Grant by following her on Twitter @mrsjessicagrant.

ENERGY AT WORK

As John Wooden and Steve Jamison describe in *Wooden on Leadership* (2005), teams feel and experience the leader's level of energy and enthusiasm. If these qualities are absent from the leader, she simply cannot expect it from others or find it among them. Energy and enthusiasm are palpable throughout an organization, or not. A lack of energy is also obvious within an organization, as the general culture is tiring and difficult. Energy, as a force within any organizational culture, is not something that we can ignore as leaders when we make efforts to strategically plan or engage our staff. All of the key drivers of success for a school or business are leveraged by the energy from the leader and the people doing the work. Cultivating a culture that is inspiring and motivating, one of pride and joy, requires intensity and fortitude. This type of leadership elicits several different thoughts and emotions when people describe a working experience where energy is at the core. Movement, vitality, liveliness, passion, and connectedness are just a short list of the words that people use to describe an energetic workplace. The bottom line is that energy is synonymous with action.

Leaders who energize the organization take clear and deliberate action as they pursue the vision they set for themselves and the workers. Action-oriented leaders understand the fundamental principles of energy. Energy is always available, we merely need to take action to harness it productively. And when we use energy as a means to achieve our desired goal, we gather more force and, in turn, create momentum.

"When energy is transferred to an object by the action of a force, the transferred energy is called work" (Jaffe & Taylor, 2018, p. 15). When we put this in the context of our "work" experiences and leadership, we begin to understand how greater amounts of energy in the workplace create better results for any given group of people or project. In other words, our work is the application of our internal capacity (energy) to complete any given task based on the energy we transfer to it and to one another. When we learn to control this force, we can begin to produce more of it and accelerate our working experiences together.

There are two types of energy of which leaders need to be mindful so that they can channel them within the working environment. The first is our mental energy, which is the output of our intellectual abilities based on our emotional state. The second is our physical energy, which is the exertion of our physiological being based on our overall health. Both are important to sharpen, and great leaders know that the emotional and physical well-being of the people in the organization are chief concerns in terms of quality outcomes.

Leaders who keep the mental and physical wellness of their employees in the forefront of the work are able to reap the benefits from the culture they cultivate. The primary outcome is higher rates of retention since there is an overall enthusiasm that comes from talented, energized people who are experiencing consistent results. A quick tip on this for educators is in the use of programs, such as TeacherFit, whose mission reads as such: "Changing teachers' lives through health and fitness in order to allow them to impact their students."

TeacherFit is an example of a focused program for both mental and physical agility, combining meditation with workout sessions so that teachers can be their best in life and work. School leaders who know the value of energy at work invest in not only the professional learning experiences that teachers need to improve their technical abilities but also the emotional and physical readiness necessary to do the job well from day to day. When we invest in energy, we profit from it through stronger engagement and increased commitment.

Once we understand that energy in the workplace is always present and requires our attention, as leaders we can use it to supply a constant stream of positivity. Energy is uniquely associated with motion and action, and because it is neither created nor destroyed, leaders can employ its awesome power to create momentum, increase productivity, and elicit positive feelings for ourselves and others. It may sound "Pollyanna," but if you've ever experienced the synergy in working with a team who truly generates zeal, you've realized the benefit in harnessing energy to create positive emotions.

The differentiating mark of great leaders is their ability to productively use energy to create a place that lifts the entire organization to achieve results each day with enthusiasm and purpose. This works in contrast to leaders who muddle in only setting policies, creating rules, and managing compliance. Energy production as a leadership competency may sound like a stretch, but the real difference between success and failure is always our attitude and how we approach any given scenario. As Michael Fullan and Joanne Quinn write in *Coherence*,

> Structure and strategy are not enough. The solution requires the individual and collective ability to build shared meaning, capacity, and commitment to action. When large numbers of people have a deeply understood sense of what needs to be done—and see their part in achieving that purpose—coherence emerges and powerful things happen. (2016, p. 1)

This power, we believe, is born from the positive energy that improves our emotional state, which in turn strengthens our mental agility, thereby leveraging more energy. The same is true in the physical realm, and leaders who care about energy at work must focus on it for the sake of the organization and the people they serve.

Before you disregard the power of positive energy as a foundational tool that is within your control, and that you are responsible for working toward, consider the world-famous Pike Place Fish Market in Seattle. Most people don't realize that the whole notion and labeling as "world famous" was a last-ditch effort to salvage a business that was near bankruptcy due to its venture into the wholesale side of the industry. The owner, John Yokoyama, took a leap of faith and hired a consultant he couldn't afford, but, in the end, they created a vision to be world famous.

This vision generated the level of energy and enthusiasm necessary to actually achieve world fame. The critical difference-maker, though, is not just his belief in a vision that was willed into existence but that it was fused with an unrelenting commitment that our energy has the potential to create for each person we encounter.

One important aspect for Yokoyama was believing in creativity as an input for greater energy output. When we give people space to be themselves, they don't then need external motivating factors. "We view people in a different way. People are not objects to be motivated or persuaded into action. Fundamentally, people are creative beings" (Yokoyama & Michelli, 2004, p. 23). People should not be looked at as "objects" that complete an assigned function but rather forms of energy to be harnessed and unleashed as a creative and productive force within the organization. The Pike Place Fish Market is an example of energy at work. The more energy the market produces, the more energy the employees exude, the more energy they receive. The cycle continues.

This belief in human creativity, and the force that we can create within an organization, is critical in the world of education where energy and inspiration are paramount to success. In a top-down era of accountability, compliance, and assessment-driven targets, we need to be able to see past the constraints so that we can empower educators to once again take ownership of their craft and actively pursue the most creative and proven strategies for student learning. This is a call to action for a refocus that requires a relinquishing of control from the leader to actively reinvigorate the staff, generating energy to sustain the level of effort necessary to reach the vision of the organization.

When we take talented people and we stoke their enthusiasm, the result is always an energy that is almost impossible to extinguish. When energy is high and flowing in the right direction, people feel it and they want to remain connected to it as a source of personal satisfaction with work and life. This means that school and district leaders must place a continual focus on staff well-being as well as the creative space for them to take on new roles. And, it only works if the leader models the way.

Delegation

In Jessica Grant's inspiring story that we used to introduce this chapter, she didn't become the new teachers' mentor to somehow save the day; instead, she empowered her more seasoned teachers to do the work, and they, in turn, became energized by it. One major reason for this is that she delegated important tasks to them, and they realized the critical value that each member of the team has, especially when it comes to the retention of our newest teachers. Jessica knew that in order to sustain high levels of energy from everyone, she needed to ensure that all of the teachers felt valued. The new teachers felt the value of the additional time and resources being allocated for their success, and the experienced teachers felt the value of their needed expertise for new staff.

One of the key ways to value an employee is by creating opportunities for them to add value. We continue to see the cyclical nature of this work—when we value employees by providing space for them to add value, they feel that value and crave more experiences to demonstrate it. In Jane Dutton's, *Energize Your Workplace* (2003), she describes the importance of connections and how, through our actions, we "till the ground," which creates meaningful work relationships that are empowering for the people around us.

The law of the harvest surfaces, again, as we invest time on the important particulars of the day to produce tremendous results in the future. One interesting way to take advantage of Dutton's concepts in schools and districts is by leveraging the often-forgotten tool of management known as *delegation*. Dutton describes how the "act of delegation is actually an act of trust . . . the tough question is whether to give away control and responsibility when it counts" (p. 90).

In education, we can be lured into the belief that the leader must handle all of the important tasks, especially when teachers are mostly left to the business of teaching. But great schools are places where everyone adds tremendous value, which means everyone must do something beyond their "regular" assignment. Interestingly, these additional roles are precisely the ones that keep us coming back for more.

The difficulty lies within our own ability to both give up control and identify the people who are best suited for a particular function. The benefit in relinquishing control is not only that it strengthens trust, it also creates a new kind of enthusiasm for the individual who accepts the responsibility. When we are working to motivate and retain teachers, our most effective method is through meaningful engagement and that engagement is demonstrated in the form of delegation of an important task.

As leaders, we often wonder why some people are more self-motivated and self-regulated than others, but we notice that the most self-motivated individuals have typically "delegated" and accepted important responsibilities themselves. That's called *self-delegation*, but not all people do that naturally. And leaders are more likely to self-delegate when they should be looking to others for help. Service is not always accomplished through doing the work that others can do for themselves and the team.

When a new task arises at school, we often think to support the team by completing the task to support their needs, but, in reality, the best way to energize others is to delegate the task. In doing so, we perpetuate a sense of "self-connectedness" to the work, which promotes new levels of energy. The alternative is when the team sees others, particularly management, as having a specialized role in servicing them. It's counterintuitive but, the more we do for others, the more likely they'll do less for the team and themselves, disconnecting them from the work and squandering their enjoyment.

In a culture that retains teachers in their positions, it's not likely (or not only) the teaching position that is producing the retention. It's more likely "everything else" that the culture provides, including key tasks that have been delegated to the teachers who stay the longest. Even when we reminisce about our own experiences in school, we typically recall the teachers we liked best not only by what they created as an experience in the classroom but their involvement in some other aspect of our lives. When talented teachers are enthusiastic about an initiative, program, or purposeful task, their energy spikes in all other areas of their work.

It's wonderful when people are focused and self-motivated enough to implement their own new ideas or pick up an additional function of the school. But leaders who capitalize on workplace energy know that they need to engage everyone in the school community. They rely on delegation as a tool to empower people, and they model energy and empowerment from their own position.

Modeling

The superstar teachers who we want to stay on our team are the ones who continually contribute to the organization in unique ways outside the classroom. Their contributions include and extend beyond extracurricular activities and after school enrichment responsibilities. True delegation means that teachers hold leadership positions or have leadership responsibilities where they actually help to guide and to navigate the ship.

To build this type of environment, one where teachers want to be and are involved in ways other than their teaching roles, requires the leader to exemplify the characteristics she desires from the team. In other words, leaders must consistently display the behaviors they want from the team. In schools, this always starts with being positive and maintaining a confident outlook toward making a difference in the lives of all students. Not only does positivity empower others, it impacts the entire organization.

Barbara Fredrickson, an author of several books on positivity, identifies key results that organizations experience when the leader models positivity. She says that "positive emotions fuel resilience," "positive emotions may produce optimal functioning in organizations," and the "leader's positive emotions are contagious" (Fredrickson, 2019). As such, any leader who wants to build a team of positive people must first model positivity herself.

And modeling doesn't stop at positivity. Great leaders focus on their actions as a catalyst for changing the behaviors of the people around them. They take full ownership because they know that the organization and the people in it are a reflection of their behaviors. Through our research and experiences, we've identified three top behaviors that leaders must display as contagions for a school and district: positivity, energy, and ownership.

When leaders keep a positive outlook, demonstrate high levels of energy and enthusiasm, and take ownership of both good and bad outcomes, others will do the same. We've found that these three, above all else, are the most contagious leadership behaviors to model. There are other strategies for developing key leadership characteristics in the people you serve, but for positivity, energy, and ownership, modeling is the best way to go.

In the following "Technical Tip," we take a look into the leadership lessons of Navy SEAL Jocko Willink with his willingness to accept full ownership of a mission gone wrong in Ramadi. His actions as a leader generate tremendous positivity for his team. He is able to energize the "troops" by not only accepting responsibility for the situation they're in but by being optimistic about what the future holds as an ultimate outcome. The point is that he leads by example. He knows that his actions communicate what he expects. Willink is a real person, but for dramatic effect, let's consider Tom Hanks' character in *Saving Private Ryan*.

He was humble yet brave, pragmatic yet optimistic. He modeled what he wanted from his men. Not only did they follow his lead but they looked up to him with immense admiration. Because he modeled what he expected from them, they carried out the mission with energy and strength. Only later in the story do we find out that Hanks' character was a schoolteacher back at home.

Breaking thresholds and reaching new heights, pushing into territories yet unexplored, is daunting work. Through great modeling, though, people can "pick up many things: ethics, values and standards; style, beliefs and attitudes; methods and procedures" (Hart, 2010). When we model a standard of excellence, through our actions and attitudes, we get, in return, a greater contribution to the school and a far more committed workforce. When we push forward by communicating our positive outlook, by demonstrating an energetic and agile mental and physical state, and by taking ownership of every circumstance we find, the team will be much more likely to do the same.

TECHNICAL TIP: OWN IT

"Leadership is influence, nothing more and nothing less" (Maxwell, 1998 p. 20). How well a leader energizes her team to accomplish something incredible rests on her ability to influence them. The challenge is that leading people toward a desired goal requires a constant and deliberate effort to create a culture of enthusiasm. It necessitates that the leader develop a support system by harnessing the power of delegation and modeling the way. Most importantly, the work of leading must be "owned" by the school leader for others to do the same in their domain.

Taking ownership and accepting full responsibility of the organization is the hallmark of all great leaders. US Navy SEAL, Jocko Willink, in his book *Extreme Ownership* (2015), gives an astounding account of a military operation that went wrong in the Mala'ab District, Ramadi, Iraq. The author describes how amid the awful weather conditions, a literal blanket of fog, the situation was worsened by their own "confusion, inaccurate information, broken communications, and mayhem" (p. 18). The initial stage of the operation was considered a failure because one Iraqi ally soldier was killed, others wounded, and a US soldier was badly hurt.

Despite the unpredictability of warfare, operations like the one Willink describes are successful based on planning and execution; this mission went bad because of mistakes in that process. Reflecting back on the mission revealed various opportunities that could have improved the outcome, but the bigger realization that Jocko made was that he was in charge of the mission and, however painful it was to admit, the full responsibility rested on his shoulders. Granted, everyone plays a role, but, as he writes, "it was a heavy burden to bear. But it was true, I was the leader. I was in charge and I was responsible" (Willink & Babin, 2015 p. 28).

Although school leaders are not on the front lines of active combat, many would argue that we are on the front lines of saving our students' lives on a real and regular basis. Schools have evolved, becoming the community hub for all things related to care and support for the well-being of children (and often their entire families). This requires schools to function beyond teaching and learning and, at many times, outside of their expertise. Students come to us with a host of needs that demand incredible time and resources. Simply put, many students do not come to school "learning ready."

The harsh realities of their circumstances leave them unattended, deprived, hungry, and sometimes desperate for attention. Consider the great equalizer, poverty, which doesn't discriminate and has proven to be more influential regarding student performance than gestational drug use (Children's Hospital of Philadelphia, 2013). For schools to succeed amid all of the challenges and to retain incredible teachers for a winning team, they must take ownership of every circumstance that they face. To do so, we offer a simple tool so that you can consistently reinforce your efforts to own every situation with a positive mindset and the energy needed to tackle the challenges of the day—*OWN IT*.

- *Operationalize* every aspect of the support system.
  - To operationalize all functions within your workplace, you must use "systems thinking" to develop a standardized process for the way you tackle common issues.
    Example: Each year families struggle to provide for Thanksgiving. The school typically steps in with support, but a more systematized approach can be used by engaging the team, delegating roles, and using it as an opportunity to be a *H3 Giving School* for the entire community.
- *Wrestle* with every nuance.
  - The devil is always in the details. The specifics and technical aspects of the work are always what diminish the flow of things. When your team grapples with the minor details during the planning phase of any initiative or event, they'll execute better, feel better about the product, and gain more pride.
    Example: The seating arrangements for the school play can be a disastrous experience for parents or one of excellence and service.
- *Nurture* each relationship to build a level of comfort for vulnerability and care.
  - Listen to your staff and give them the great satisfaction of your time. Allow them to feel comfortable in sharing their mistakes and mishaps. Too often people either cover up their mistakes for fear that they look weak or because there isn't time for reflection built into the day. Leaders who "own it" nurture mistakes as learning opportunities.
    Example: At each meeting, build in time for people to recall a recent mistake they made. Either let them share how they fixed the problem or turn the problem over to the team for support.
- *Influence* the team in positive ways.
  - Make a social investment in your team. Recall the second part of the *Habitual Happiness Highpoints* (H3) process. You can

positively influence each team member by creating space to learn about their social lives and by putting together time for the team to "just share."

Example: You should know the names of your teachers' kids and what they're up to in life.

- *Trust* your system and your leadership team.
  - ◦ Great teams rely on each other and work together based on trust. Put people in key roles to be a source of knowledge, encouragement, and inspiration and then get out of their way. If you do the O, W, N, and I aspects of OWN IT, the T is where you place your trust that the team has a system, knows the details that matter most, feels free to share mistakes, and follows your lead in a positive way. Trust that. Leaders who truly "own it" turn it over to others to own.

    Example: You might feel like it's your job to play a huge role in the student scheduling process. But if you have systems and people in place, get out of their way and trust them to do the work in accordance with your vision.

Each aspect of OWN IT is vital to retaining top talent by providing them with a stable and supportive environment at school. The acronym is a simple reminder to consider the key areas that need your attention and focus throughout the year. If we want to retain our quality people, we have to do far more than hand them a set of keys, a login password, and an ID badge. Implementing OWN IT into your routine is a great way to normalize the process of support. The dichotomy of owning it, though, is in letting go. Leaders who "own it" best are the ones who demonstrate their ownership by empowering the team to "own it." When we model OWN IT, everyone owns it.

GUIDING QUESTIONS

1. What strategies or programs are you using to focus on staff mental and physical well-being?
2. Which aspect of the work you're doing can be delegated to someone on the team to create energy and enthusiasm for him or her?
3. How are we modeling and demonstrating the principles of OWN IT as a school or district.

Chapter Five

Accelerated Acclimation for New Teachers

Exploring, experimenting, learning: this is the way we're designed to live. And work, too (Cable, 2018).

NEW HIRE SUPPORT

Hopefully the benefits of splitting your hiring practices into a *before*, *during*, and *after* structure are clear. Successful schools always position themselves for sustainability so let's assume that your reputation is stellar, your hiring practices are innovative, and your retention rates are higher than ever. You're performing at the top of your game, but you still have openings due to natural attrition, such as retirements, and teacher advancements into administration. Even if your turnover rates are low, most schools hire someone new each year and need a structured acclimation program.

New people must be treated as precious cargo for three main reasons: 1) They leave. "National studies of teacher retention indicate that around 20–30% of new teachers leave the profession within the first five years" (Guha, Hyler, & Darling-Hammond, 2016), 2) It's expensive. Schools lose between $1 and $2.2 billion a year to attrition (Schaffhauser, 2014), and 3) Student achievement. "Research finds that high rates of turnover harm student achievement" (Carver-Thomas & Darling-Hammond, 2017). But, being "new" is not restricted to just those teachers entering the profession. It also includes teachers new to your school and district.

It's critical to consider anyone who is joining our team, even if they have several years of experience, as "new" for their first 3–5 years. The intent is to successfully acclimate and engage them within the culture. For this reason, new hires and their adjustment period should be organized into four categories for success. We provide the categories here and then key strategies for addressing them in the "Leadership Team Activity" at the end of this chapter.

First, *organizational culture* is a key factor in supporting and motivating staff for both retention and fit. This means that you need a new employee integration strategy. One study found that 70 percent of newly hired people cited issues with a lack of understanding about general company norms and acceptable practices (Byford, Watkins, & Triantogiannis, 2017).

Because all schools come with a different set of organizational dynamics, norms, and responsibilities, let alone internal networks and group dynamics, new hires can find themselves alienated from the culture versus accepted and embraced by it. This creates uncertainty and doubt, which can lead to anxiety and increased stress, a detrimental situation that will adversely affect teacher performance by spilling into the classroom, impacting student achievement and job satisfaction.

Second, much like fitting in on any new team, *socialization* and peer support are critical to the success of a newbie. It's difficult to break into already established peer groups, and teams of teachers can be among the worst, often unintentionally, at providing a newcomer with the necessary space to fit in. The scary part is that there are so many early influences on a new teacher; you can't allow for the slightest void, leaving any of the new person's influences to chance.

The goal is for the staff to be overwhelmingly positive and inviting, but we know that negativity and cultural toxicity are common and continually need to be addressed. The last thing you need is for your new hire to find her way into a negative social peer group. Acclimating your new teacher through the use of a positive teacher leader is vital because "a negative teacher-leader . . . can convince other teachers to be negative as well" (Whitaker, 2015, p. 6). Bottom line, you have to be strategic during the onboarding process.

Third, every new person brings their own set of *past experiences* and skills to the team. Much of any new hire's expertise cannot be learned through the interview process. Although we call for new and innovative ways to select candidates, and we provide strategies for making gains in this area, we realize that new people bring a ton of value that you can't see until they're on the team. Conversely, the opposite may be true as well. Sometimes, you're excited about a new hire, all the references check out perfectly, and when they come aboard, you quickly realize that there are areas that need immediate attention. Worse yet, you may not come to this realization until your first observation, which may not happen until a third or half of the year is over.

> Sometimes it happens that a candidate who had the right credentials, seemed to fly through the interview process, and had lovely references turns out to be an unexpected problem after hiring. If it hasn't happened to you yet, consider yourself lucky, because only 19% of new hires are considered fully successful . . . and by the 18-month point 46% are deemed failures. (Kislik, 2018)

The truth is that you don't have time to figure out if a new teacher isn't working out, which is precisely why research suggests that our attrition problem is seriously detrimental for student achievement (Carver-Thomas & Darling-Hammond, 2017). Structures and supports need to be established so that not only is the individual receiving the attention they deserve, there is also a way for you to quickly determine how well the person is adjusting and performing.

Fourth, school leaders need a way to communicate an *expectation alignment* with new hires. An expectation alignment is a calibration between what the school leader expects as business-as-usual (BAU) and what an employee expects as BAU. In education, we don't talk enough about BAU or ROI (return on investment) or KPIs (key performance indicators). We are not suggesting that schools should be run like businesses or that schools don't have their own methods to determine effectiveness; that mentality isn't helpful or productive. What we do suggest is that there are several management structures that establish productivity and denote success practices from which schools can benefit. For example, we believe that every school leader can benefit from the powerful work of business icons like Peter Drucker.

In any event, leaders often set expectations that evolve over time. New hires have no way of knowing what those expectations are unless you have established a clear strategy for communicating them. Byford, Watkins, and Triantogiannis (2017) call this type of assimilation "accelerated integration" and it can range from "team-building workshops" to "deep-dive discussions."

New hires, those in their first five years with your school, are an employee group unlike any other. They are susceptible to turnover at greater rates, and they're easily impressionable in the right or wrong direction. As you build your winning team, it's imperative that you take a strategic approach with new teachers. The good news is that some of the teacher turnover equation is well within your control.

"Administrative support is often the top reason teachers identify for leaving or staying in the profession, or in a given school, outweighing even salary considerations for some teachers" (Podolsky, Kini, Bishop, & Darling-Hammond, 2016). We believe that this type of support should go to your most vulnerable staff first. New teachers should have quality onboarding and "day-one" programs that acclimate them to a teaching and learning environment that is bursting with energy and is a fun place to work for everyone on the team. As we discussed in *Building a Winning Team*, you can't leave your reputation to chance and your hiring process should be well-established. Here, we spend this chapter and the next totally focused on new hires because after they're on board, they need serious time and attention.

Onboarding

If you work in a school, and you have a system for onboarding teachers and other staff members that lasts for more than their first week, take a second and applaud yourself now. According to research conducted by the Alliance for Excellent Education (2004), only one percent of teachers are being provided with quality induction programming. And, worse yet, onboarding programs are often limited to a week before school starts and rarely meet the needs that new staff members demand as they start a new school year.

It used to be that onboarding was a process of just a few days, but new research shows that spending as much as a year helping new employees get up to speed in the workplace is necessary to capitalize on the skills, knowledge, and excitement they bring to the organization. (Ellis, Nifadkar, Bauer, & Erdogan, 2017)

A new hire can be just what your team needs to excel at the next level, but their impact will be limited if they are bogged down by the minutiae associated with "learning the ropes." To retain our best people, particularly our new hires, we have to create systems of support that begin on day-one and last for at least 3–5 years. Essentially, someone shouldn't be "offboarded" until they meet every criterion of the onboarding program.

The demand for companies to retain top talent is intensifying. One report suggests that employee retention is the number one issue on the minds of CEOs today—not just in the U.S., but around the world. And yet, companies often spend very little time onboarding new hires. (Carucci, 2018)

One consideration with onboarding is the price of programming, but it's far more of an expense to lose a staff member, which is costing districts up to $20,000 per teacher (Carver-Thomas & Darling-Hammond, 2017). Fortunately, quality onboarding at the school level can be very affordable and incredibly beneficial.

In fact, one benefit of onboarding programs is that they can motivate and retain *current* employees. Because "only 34% of teachers are engaged in their job" (McFeely, 2018), onboarding has the potential to provide social and professional support for lead teachers as well as new people. "Effective onboarding programs have the dual purpose of supporting both new employees and hiring managers [or teacher leaders] through socialization and professional support" (Ellis, Nifadkar, Bauer, & Erdogan, 2017). When we engage staff, especially teacher leaders, in the process of onboarding, it always results in a win-win. That said, for onboarding to be effective, it must start on day-one.

Day-One

First and foremost, day-one for a new hire cannot be the same day that every other teacher returns to work. Day-one is a marquee moment for new hires, and when done well, it sets the stage for a standard of excellence for the rest of the year and likely even their entire career. New staff need to begin at least a few days prior to the day that everyone else comes back from summer break.

First, teachers care deeply about the importance of planning, preparing, and organizing. Introducing them to their new space, new materials, and new peers all on the same day, when everyone else is scrambling to get settled before students arrive, prevents them from receiving the attention they need and deserve. Teachers need time in their classrooms to start the school year effectively, and new staff need additional time or they will be subjected to the compounding effect of trying to manage all of their responsibilities amid already seemingly hectic conditions. The preparation time that they are afforded creates tremendous gratitude and will pay dividends in the long-run.

Second, take time to connect and greet every new hire on day-one. Formally or informally, stop by to say hello to every new teacher on their first day, on the first day when all staff are back at school, and then again sometime during the first week with students. This may sound like a simple thing to do, but the first few days back are jammed, and you can easily get to the end of the day when everyone is packed and gone without having taken valuable time to invest in the supporting relationship that new teachers need. The important fact is that teachers "who feel the most supported by their school leaders are least likely to leave their schools or teaching altogether" (Carver-Thomas & Darling-Hammond, 2017). Your support starts on day-one, even if it's just a smiling face and handshake to say "thank you for being here, we are looking forward to great things."

Third, set a meeting with each new hire for their second week of school. Take 30 minutes to sit with them to hear their thoughts about how the year began. Create a list of questions that require them to reflect and be ready to listen. It's amazing what you might find out. When we started to implement this in our schools, we learned about a lack of computer access, keycard problems for entry into the building, and other common problems that can be frustrating and demoralizing but easily fixed.

New hires are almost always reluctant to discuss their needs in the first few days of their new experiences, which is why discussing their onboarding experience, even the most mundane issues, must be intentional. Providing a smooth transition into a new job goes a long way for motivation and retention down the road and supports a greater degree of engagement on an immediate basis. One business study revealed that employees "spent nearly three times as much time collaborating with their team as those who did not have a one-on-one [in the first week of employment, and] . . . employees who spend more time collaborating have higher favorability about belonging" on the team (Klinghoffer, Young, & Liu, 2018). An early feeling of engagement creates better long-term outcomes, including retention.

The faster you can acclimate your new hires, the more support they will experience and the greater likelihood that they'll be engaged and committed to the school. Motivation is critical to the success of any organization, but the issue is that two-thirds of our teaching workforce does not feel engaged at work (McFeely, 2018). This can be changed, but it has to happen immediately upon hiring new staff, whether they are new to the profession or new to our environment.

More than anything, it takes leadership, but "leadership" can't be the sole responsibility of one person. Schools need leadership teams to drive the success of any initiative or program, especially if we're going to retain people because of a positive working culture. That's exactly why it's so important that you have an "Accelerated School Acclimation Program" embedded within your culture.

LEADERSHIP TEAM ACTIVITY—ACCELERATED SCHOOL ACCLIMATION PROGRAM (ASAP)

To complement the onboarding and day-one activities, we offer an *Accelerated School Acclimation Program* (ASAP) that we hope you'll adapt for your school. Followed by its four-part system, you'll find the final key to motivating both new and current teachers in the next chapter: mentoring. Note that these strategies are not simply for new hires; putting them into practice in a team environment will be motivational and inspirational for everyone.

If you want to accelerate the acclimation process for new teachers in your school or district, the best way is to engage your teacher leaders as the facilitators, advisers, and coaches. Yes, the principal plays a key role, but just because "administrative support is often the top reason teachers identify for leaving" (Podolsky, Kini, Bishop, & Darling-Hammond, 2016), doesn't mean that all of the work of teacher induction is left to the principal.

Fullan (2014, 2019), an exceptional educational leadership thinker and prolific writer on the topic, consistently reports that great leaders know two things: they cannot do everything themselves and leadership requires a nuanced approach. In other words, delegation and distributed autonomy are fundamental along with the idea that canned, wholesale, replicable programs and processes have serious limitations. We need well-informed teams of people with an adaptable and agile style about them who are ready to use a multitude of proven methods for leading a school forward.

In the case of new teacher orientation and induction, we're calling for a four-part plus one systems approach. The first four parts are our "Accelerated School Acclimation Program" (ASAP) and the "plus one" is a mentoring program that adds value for new teachers, which we explain further in chapter 6. Take note that these leadership team strategies are meant to be modified as you see fit for your school culture.

1. *Culture Class.* "An excellent culture is critical to the success of any organization" (Casas, 2017). Every school and district has its own unique culture, which consists of norms, behaviors, and a framework of some sort that is built on an explicit or implicit set of core principles. The critical notion about culture is that if you don't create the culture you want and expect as the leader, and you leave it to chance—one will be created that you may or may not like. New staff are vulnerable to the aspects of the school culture that are both positive and negative, pulling them in either direction. The key is to facilitate a positive direction by using your school champions who serve on your leadership team. This becomes a primary way in which you communicate and reinforce cultural norms and expectations. We call it "culture class."

   The first step of culture class is to meet with your leadership team to review the school vision and core values. You can incorporate your archetype of a teacher into this conversation as well. You might even list a set of culture principles. Casas (2017) introduces "champion for all students," "expect excellence," "carry the banner," and "be a merchant of hope" as his four core areas of culture (p. 14–15). But, even without cultural principles of this kind, your vision, core values, and archetype will serve as the basis for the class. A few key members of the team will likely emerge during the conversation about the concept.

Your goal is to identify two to three teacher leaders to lead a conversation with new hires after school, centered on the culture of your school—how teachers are expected to carry themselves, how they can positively contribute to the culture, and what they can expect from the school in return. The team can work together to brainstorm scenarios, readings, and other teaching tools for the class. The key is to convey the message within the first few weeks of school. This is all part of ASAP for new teachers so that they become comfortable in their new setting as fast as possible. The quicker they acclimate, the better they'll perform for their students. Your job is to lead the conversation, delegate responsibility, and schedule a time and place.

2. *Social Committee.* In studies about new hire acclimation, "feeling socially accepted was a key factor in newcomer success" (Ellis, Nifadkar, Bauer, & Erdogan, 2017). For this reason, a formal Social Committee is indispensable. Many schools have a committee, like a Sunshine Committee, that plans birthday and wedding showers, among other celebrations. In *Passionate Leadership* (2020) we advocate that you can't stop there with celebrations, and here we are taking this one step further with the use of a new staff social induction.

Social induction is not hazing or indoctrination, just in case we're misunderstood; it's quite the opposite. You need one or two members of your leadership team to be the chair of the Social Committee, using the Leadership Team as the driver for the committee's charge. At a minimum, this committee will plan social events, during school (such as potluck luncheons) and after school (such as family bowling night) and other fun social interactions for staff meetings, etc. The key is to strategically ensure that new teachers are woven into the social fabric of the school, creating a sense of belonging to your winning team. The more that one group can create belonging for another, the more likely it is that they'll feel it for themselves.

3. *A Monitoring and Support Plan.* One trend is that many people are joining the teaching profession through alternative routes to the classroom more than ever, with one in four new teachers entering the workforce from diverse backgrounds outside of traditional teacher preparation programs (Carver-Thomas & Darling-Hammond, 2017). While this is a good thing, "teachers with little preparation tend to leave at rates two to three times as high as those who have had

comprehensive preparation before they enter" (Sutcher, Darling-Hammond, & Carver-Thomas, 2016).

That said, administrators often think of evaluations as an observation tool and a support mechanism, yet the teacher may not see them in the same light. Even if a new teacher is observed between three and five times per year in the classroom and is receiving feedback, the observations are typically viewed by the new teacher solely as performance evaluations, which they don't necessarily connect with support. This is primarily because the same tool and process can be used as evidence of poor performance.

As an alternative, new teachers need additional support from other staff and different types of visits to their classrooms. You need a plan for teacher leaders, department chairs, and grade level leaders to monitor and support new hire instructional practices. With your leadership team, you can develop a comprehensive plan to visit new teachers as often as twice per week for support and informal feedback. This process adds support and is not directly tied to a teacher's performance appraisal. The key is to mix both teacher leader and supervisor feedback. If you wait for supervisory evaluation systems to guide your conversations with new teachers, you're bound to lose them, especially if they're struggling in areas that need support rather than judgment.

4. *New Teacher Monthly Meetings.* "A new employee's manager is one of the most important people in the onboarding experience, and gaining this person's support may directly improve or undermine a new hire's chances of succeeding" (Ellis, Nifadkar, Bauer, & Erdogan, 2017). This is the last component of the ASAP and it falls on the school leader to implement. For this aspect of the program, you'll need to gather input from your team about the needs that they are seeing for new teacher stability and retention, but you must then hold your own monthly after-school meetings for your new staff.

The meeting style may take on different forms, but the goal is that the participants' experience is supportive while reinforcing high leverage instructional practices with proven outcomes. The administration doesn't always have to lead the sessions, but they do always need to attend to add value as the leader. Topics can vary, from a particular instructional strategy to dealing with difficult parents, but they should be ongoing and supportive of the needs that your leadership team identifies as gaps in new teacher assimilation to your culture.

For an ASAP to be successful, it must be a standing agenda item for the leadership team to answer critical questions about new teacher supports, which also sparks engagement with any current staff member who is willing to step up to support the school. But ASAP doesn't stop there; it has a *plus one* model to it. The final piece of an Accelerated School Acclimation Program is a quality mentoring component. We pull this out into a special section because it's unlike the other four components. It's about a network of support and professional collaboration beyond meeting times and social networking.

The first four components are about *the person*; mentoring is about people, as well, but it's also about honing in on *the work*. Mentoring offers comfort and support, but it should also develop the new hire in terms of their effectiveness. The goal is the transfer of expertise from the mentor to the mentee in terms of masterful teaching. "Instructional mentoring is effective when it is consistent and based on an explicit vision of good teaching as well as an understanding of teacher learning" (Feiman-Nemser, 2001). Mentoring pushes beyond counseling; great mentors can also be incredible coaches.

STANDING OUT—WHAT OWNERSHIP LOOKS LIKE IN ACTION—ANGELA SOCORSO

One of the most powerful attributes of our home state, Delaware, is the amazing relationships that we've developed among the professionals in different schools and districts. Delaware provides a unique connectedness because even though folks reside in different counties, we are only a short drive away from one another. Despite being small, the state is incredibly diverse. The northern part of the state is home to the city of Wilmington with all of the elements of any urban area, and the southern portion of the state is made up of both coastal and rural areas, including in its commerce some of the leading chicken exporters in the country.

This diversity within such a small geographical area allows for the blending of ideas, which gives rise to powerful programs of work that are easily shared and replicated by neighboring partners. With great pride, we want to introduce you to one of our Delaware friends, Angela Socorso. Angie is the Supervisor of Educator Effectiveness in the Smyrna School District, and, as you are about to learn, she is doing fantastic work to support the students and teachers in Delaware.

Angie, a veteran educator, is very sensitive to the needs of new teachers. In her district she realized the need to develop a program to support new teachers and to onboard them in a productive and fruitful manner. She created time to embed the coaching necessary to reinforce the vision of the district so that new teachers were acclimated to their important roles.

To bring this to life, she decided to creatively capture an image of the district's mascot, and what she deemed as the Eagles' New Educator Support Team (NEST) was born. Angie told us about the initial meeting she held to begin the work, which focused on three things: reflection, intention, and connection.

After Angie started the meeting and dove into the first activity, the initial mentoring session never progressed beyond that point. Their time together became only about the sharing of experiences. Despite a full agenda that she had planned for mentoring, Angie deviated and tapped into the power of stories. Each participant had to describe a positive and challenging experience that they had encountered thus far in the year.

Angie told us that the sharing became a well of mentoring opportunities and that there were "many thoughts and reflections from the group, many tears, and many stories of support. It was a great session of connection." Angie continued to reflect that her great takeaway, a revelation she called it, was "the fact that the teachers are so passionate and want to do a great job, but they feel like failures when they don't make an immediate breakthrough." The NEST allowed them to comfort one another and to build their confidence to keep going.

The power in the participants' testimonies uncovers what we've known about the consciousness of teachers, which is that they care immensely for the development of the whole child. They so desire for their students to experience success that when their students face hurdles, challenges, and frustrations, they too bear that burden.

But great mentoring programs offer support and perspective. They always shed light on the bigger picture and the positive outcomes of our work. Angie shared that, "tears of joy came from one teacher who has already seen growth in a little guy who wouldn't even pick up a book to read during the first few weeks."

It's these successes that fill our hearts and remind us of the importance of what we do. They strengthen our resolve for when the inevitable struggles seem insurmountable, when student progress is delayed and our every solution and available accommodations aren't proving effective. Mentoring sessions create time and space for reflection, allowing us to be explicit with our intentions and make connections beyond the classroom. The NEST provides the structure to give teachers a voice, to reinforce sound practices, to offer skillful guidance, and to empower new teachers as they find their foothold within the profession.

Although this program is in its infancy, it is tailored to fit the unique demands of the new teachers while serving each of their individual needs. We also want to highlight that in her role, Angie essentially serves as the lead mentor in her district. She is a mentor of mentors. Not only does she provide the opportunity for new educators to gather at the NEST, she models this level of support for other leaders who act as mentors to new staff. She demonstrates the commitment and ownership that is necessary for new educators to thrive and the time that is required for leaders to build a winning team.

The NEST program will meet throughout the year to cover key aspects of teaching and learning for the newest Eagles. Angie revealed that next on the agenda is "knowing your why" and the importance of your personal core values in informing how you should confront various situations in life and work. You can follow Angela Socorso on Twitter @AngieSocorso.

GUIDING QUESTIONS

1. What aspects of your culture are most important to convey to new teachers to your school and district?
2. Who should be the face of your social integration and school celebration planning?
3. What new staff supports are needed as you move through each month of the school year?

Chapter Six

Quality Mentors

A strong peer mentor is not something that just happens (Brooks & Joseph, 2019, p. 97).

MENTORING PROGRAMS

New staff members bring a world of possibilities to a school. We expect them to make an immediate impact on the students and the organization. However, this requires a strong system that can unlock their potential through specific supports and needed guidance while they learn about the intricacies of their new job. Within the right culture, all of this can happen through a well-developed induction and mentoring program that relies on a network of people who strengthen the onboarding, assistance, and, ultimately, the retention of great staff.

None of this happens by accident, though, which means that it takes a well-developed mentoring plan that supports a growth-minded culture. "An impactful mentor models professionalism and creates a safe environment for a mentee. A safe environment for mentees increases their level of happiness, resulting in an increase in productivity, retention rates and overall positive feelings toward the school, colleagues, and students" (Brooks & Joseph, 2019, p. 51).

There are a few specific life events such as specialized training, background experiences, and schooling that can positively equip some new teachers above others. Experiences such as student teaching and an education within a specific content area both rate incredibly high as indicators of future success in the profession (Behrstock-Sherratt, Bassett, Olson, & Jacques, 2014). And, another very important indicator of success is having a quality mentor.

Arguably, mentoring may be the most important in-the-field, on-the-job support that new hires can receive during the formative years of their tenure. The first few years as a new teacher are difficult and the stressors can range widely, including anything from understanding the online learning management system to dealing with resistant students. Strong mentors create opportunities for new hires to find their way and overcome current and future challenges in their careers. And, the rewards of mentorship are not solely reserved for new employees.

We often think of the mentee as the primary beneficiary of the mentoring relationship, but as we learned through Jessica Grant's story, the mentor can benefit as well. The relationship builds a stronger staff member in the mentor as they take ownership of supporting an individual, which in turn supports the overall mission of the school. Great mentoring programs add value for everyone. They don't just result in retention for new teachers; they also give veteran teachers greater purpose, anchoring them within the system they are helping to create. Successful mentoring programs require several very specific structures to produce beneficial outcomes.

First, a strong program creates an immediate connection for the new person by establishing and fostering a peer relationship between the new hire and an experienced staff member. Early connections foster the feeling that the new person is fully accepted and that they belong as a member of the team, which is vital for retention in the long run. Effective programs are intentional about the relationship side of the pairing and focus on more than just the technical aspects of the job.

Quick Tip: Try to cross-pollinate between groups by having different grade levels and departments mentor outside of their typical professional network. Appreciating and respecting diversity is a key characteristic of employees feeling connected and included (O'Hara, 2014).

Second, mentoring is not just a training program, it is a process to support the new person's growth and development in the job while on the job (Tjan, 2017). It's an avenue for experienced professionals to pass on their expertise, particularly on the noninstructional, people side of the business. The Greek philosopher, Plato, acknowledged, in his work *The Republic,* that we must try to gain knowledge from those who have gone before us:

> There is nothing I like better, Cephalus, than conversing with aged men. For I regard them as travelers who have gone a journey which I too may have to go, and of whom I ought to inquire whether the way is smooth and easy or rugged and difficult. (Plato, p. 2)

Great mentors use their own and others' past experiences so that the mentee can learn from mistakes others have made and try to avoid the same pitfalls. An ideal mentoring situation is retrospective. When mentors are able to use storytelling as a teaching tool, mentees gain perspective that is greater than simply being told what to do in a given situation.

Quick Tip: Great mentors don't wait until the mentee is "in trouble" or facing a difficult challenge. They foresee potential needs and problems before they arise through actively listening, and they tell personal stories that match the learning needs of the mentee.

Third, done well and structured appropriately, mentoring may be the most effective nonthreatening strategy for new employees to seize an opportunity to learn more about themselves as professionals to become masters of their craft. Great mentors don't just "show the ropes," they facilitate reflection and learning to promote self-understanding. At the peak of the experience, they become coaches who demonstrate what mastery looks like in the classroom. They ask probing questions to prompt the mentee so that both the mentor and mentee are in a state of reflection. Through thoughtful dialogue, they push and pull in ways that gets the mentee thinking about herself, her classroom environment, and the profession as a whole.

Quick Tip: During scheduled mentoring meetings, prepare instructionally based questions for reflection rather than just responding to what the mentee's needs are at that moment.

How to deal with and manage the complexities and challenges that a new hire faces can be learned through the guidance of a well-trained mentor. The unique experiences of the mentor, their depth of knowledge regarding the system, and their ability to connect and listen effectively can be of significant value to the mentee. It is through their insight and guidance that the mentee develops the ability to navigate the waters on their own. "The best mentorships are more like the relationship between a parent and adult child than between a boss and employee. They're characterized by mutual respect, trust, shared values, and good communication" (Chopra & Saint, 2017).

A well-equipped mentor can help a person see challenges more clearly to find a solution that they wouldn't have otherwise found. A mentor listens and asks thoughtful questions, not only to better understand what is going on but also to help the mentee fully grasp what is occurring. Consider how often new teachers hear the phrase, "don't take it personally" when dealing with student misbehavior. That's not actually sage advice given that it's much easier said than done and requires a very experienced perspective on some of the most routine issues that teachers face. The truth is that teaching is a very personal experience; to not take it personally when a student acts out is counter to the natural tendencies of any teacher, especially new teachers.

That said, a veteran teacher may see a student's chronic poor attitude as a cry for help and an opportunity to galvanize resources despite potential resistance from the student and even the parents. A master teacher knows that she may be the only chance that a child has for a good education. While the novice teacher may be overwhelmed by the situation and unsure how to navigate the issue beyond submitting a discipline referral, the mentor can help her to see past that as the only resort. Or, the new teacher may even be afraid of making a mistake, rendering her unable to see how to employ the help of others to foster a structure of support for the student. Mentors change that outlook to one that is focused on using the experience for growth, producing self-efficacy in the long run.

Great mentors help their mentee see the big picture, and they are a responsive resource in times of need. From our own experience, mentors have been invaluable, particularly when consulting someone to gain perspective on what seems like an insurmountable problem or a dire situation, only to find a new avenue of clarity and possibility. Through open dialogue, mentors and mentees can come to conclusions that one or the other might not have reached without the conversation. And, for a successful program to work, there are two critical elements that need to be in place—assigning the right person for each mentee and developing an ongoing support system for mentors.

Assigning the Right Person

Consider, one immediate challenge for all teachers, which is isolation. The very nature of the four walls of a classroom reinforces a sense of solitude. It's easy for the "busyness" of the day to consume our time and, before we know it, a quarter of the year has passed with most teachers conducting lessons with very few to any visits from peers or supervisors. Couple this with our predisposed tendency as professionals to avoid guidance for fear of looking ineffective (Murad, 2014), and as a result, our new hire is potentially further removed from support. That's why the mentor/mentee relationship is important because it breaks down the walls of the school for both the new teachers and the experienced ones.

The first critical element for any successful mentoring program is found within the assignment itself. The goal is to assign the perfect match between the mentor and mentee and then to set expectations for the mentee and mentor relationship. This will help to establish the content of the meetings and to create a structure for the program. For the mentoring program to be effective, the relationship between the mentor and the mentee needs to be the right fit.

Typically, we would think that the mentor should be someone in the same department or grade level. However, this is where knowing each person and their position is vital to being able to provide the appropriate selection. The mentor can be outside of the immediate department, especially because we are working to unleash the talents of the person and essentially unveiling their best self, not necessarily building their content knowledge. The details of the job, such as orientation to the curriculum, the materials, and the rules and policies of the school, should be covered in other ways.

"Excellent mentors are intentional about taking the time to truly 'see' their mentees . . . both their authentic real selves and their ideal selves (Johnson & Smith, 2018). This approach to mentoring poses a slightly different twist; our primary focus shifts to developing the individual and having them grow as professionals to become highly effective versus filling them with information regarding the general practices so that they understand the school and its procedures. Consider the procedural aspects of their job to be essentials of the onboarding process. The mentoring program should be about their ability to fulfill their new role effectively within the structures of their new environment. As we've said, ASAP is ongoing and the mentee should be surrounded by a number of school leaders for support. This frees up time and space for the mentor to act as a coach, honing in on the specific work to be done as opposed to just meeting the natural needs of any new person.

Once the assignment is right, the mentee and mentor need to clarify what they want to achieve from the relationship. Yes, the goals of the program should be established by the school leaders and may even have to adhere to state education policies with key areas of focus already identified. However, we are referring to the relationship and commitment of those directly involved. The mentorship program cannot risk being viewed by either person as a task that needs to be completed.

Each person must identify what they will contribute and what they expect to achieve. In fact, the first meeting should be dedicated to this discussion. The value in this approach is that both the mentor and mentee have responsibilities to make the relationship work. The roles and the goals within the construct of the program need to be clearly outlined for maximum impact. To start, have the mentee take ownership of the desired outcomes by setting goals regarding what they would like to achieve. Chopra and Saint (2017) advise the mentor to:

> clarify what your mentee expects from the relationship, match it against your expectations, and reach consensus. You may have misapprehension as to the mentee's long-term goals, while the mentee may have an exaggerated notion as to what services you will provide. Such misunderstandings are costly, in terms of time and tranquility. (n.p.)

We stress this point about both the fit and the expectations because effective programs go beyond one year, which we cover further in the next section. Understanding what each person expects from the relationship also helps to clarify what the relationship entails for both parties. This allows each person to successfully navigate potential issues and problems in the future. The mentor desires a responsive individual who is willing to learn and grow, while the mentee desires a relationship that is beneficial as a value added. Any misalignment and the program will be completed for compliance with little reward for either person.

After the relationship expectations are established, the next step is to identify the details of the meetings, including the structures, times, and spaces. The school leadership team should clearly identify the overarching goals of the program, like what information gets covered and when. For example, the school may want the mentor to "observe" the mentee's classes a specific number of times.

The team may add any number of structures to the meetings, including joint lesson plan creation and specific advice on how to handle discipline matters. We like to see mentors and mentees observing one another and observing other teachers together. For success, the mentoring program needs a curriculum that is aligned to the school's vision.

Selecting the right match and setting a clear curriculum are paramount to the success of your mentoring program. We contend that doing so is the first step toward building trust. Knowing what to cover and when doesn't guarantee that the relationship will be meaningful, but it provides direction in a space that might otherwise be uncomfortable. We suggest telling the mentee and mentor why you selected them to work together and providing a written outline of a curriculum for them to follow, which can be anything from a list of topics to cover to a fully formed program of work.

When relationships are created through the right match for both the mentor and mentee and the program content is established with timelines for delivery, the next viable step is to ensure ongoing support. When we say "ongoing support" as it relates to mentoring programs, the typical response is to think of the mentee, but that's not what we are addressing. The relationship and the program are the ongoing supports for the mentee. The problem is that most programs don't provide ongoing support for the mentors.

Ongoing Support

In the *Educational Leadership* magazine article, "The Good Mentor" (1999), Rowley outlines six essential characteristics of what it means to be a "good mentor." Of the most important qualities, "the good mentor is a model of a continuous learner." They must be effective at communicating hope and optimism, able to adjust to the needs of the mentee, and committed to the role (Rowley, 1999). Above all, though, is that they need to want to learn and grow themselves. The truth is that not all new hires enter the profession with the same skills or deficits, which means that mentors need to be able to meet new teachers where they are from the outset. In addition to their ability to impart knowledge and motivate the mentee, they also need to be able to diagnose talents and uncover deficiencies quickly. In high needs schools, the need for mentors is compounded.

As we featured earlier in the book, high needs schools not only face huge obstacles, they also have the highest number of new teachers and the greatest turnover (Carver-Thomas & Darling-Hammond, 2017). This requires mentors to be highly effective in their roles so that they might stymie the revolving door that plagues these schools and their communities. For this to happen, the mentor must be equipped to handle all of the challenges that the new teacher will face and know how to guide them appropriately, even when they don't have the immediate answers.

The data suggest that much of the high teacher turnover in schools is due to a lack of support from school administration (Ingersoll & Strong, 2011). Although this sounds like it is a negative reflection on school administrators' intentions to support teachers, the fact is that they also need mentoring and support to be able to provide it. This book is a school leadership book, written as a guide for school leaders to build a sensational culture, but make no mistake that one premise of this book is that school leaders need support as well.

As we focus intently on the problems concerning teacher turnover, we often miss the mark about mentors needing mentors, coaches needing coaching, and supervisors needing supervision. We would be remiss if we didn't address the fact that quality mentoring programs have layers of support in place for the mentors themselves. That's why the second critical element for any successful mentoring program is found within the ongoing support system for the mentors, not just the mentees.

Organizations like the New Teacher Center (Goldrick, 2016) have outlined success criteria that states can adopt to increase the effectiveness of mentoring programs. Since 2012, the center has evaluated the various programs within each of the fifty states and has identified aspects of each that support new teachers and their growth. The report's findings identify "limited progress" within the area of mentoring (Goldrick, 2016). Of the various criteria that the report cites, one focus is on the need for "quality" mentoring and "multiyear support." This investment in a continuum of services is only reinforced by survey results from state teachers of the year who identified the incredible influence of mentors: "68 percent of the 55 percent of survey respondents who had an assigned or informal mentor rank[ed] it among their top three supports" (Behrstock-Sherratt et al., 2014).

This tells us that although we're making "limited progress" with mentoring overall, teachers who had effective mentors not only ranked it high as a support but turned out to do well within the profession. Being a state teacher of the year is no small feat. Hence, we conclude that the data demonstrate a new need, not necessarily for more mentoring but for better mentors.

This necessitates an ongoing support system for mentors and stronger approaches to creating multiyear programs. Multiyear support also allows for tiered support. Once new teachers gain a foothold on some of the basics of instruction, classroom management, and so on, the mentor can provide security and reassurance to pursue innovative practices and unleash the talents for which they were hired.

One plan to tackle the need for *ongoing support* for mentors, the need for a *multiyear program*, the need for *better mentors*, and the need for *more mentors* is to use *Mentoring Teams*, which can be done with your leadership team at the school level. And, this layered team approach works for both retention and motivation, serving the needs of the mentees but also the mentors.

Mentoring Teams are a way for groups of teachers to demonstrate their commitment by working with mentees and supporting one another to grow as mentors. It's a far more collaborative approach than the typical one-on-one mentoring that most programs prescribe. You can use the following activity at your next leadership team to begin the work associated with creating *Mentoring Teams* in your school.

LEADERSHIP TEAM ACTIVITY—MENTORING TEAMS

If you've read any of our previous work, you know that we're huge proponents of the power of diversity for engaging every facet of your organization. The mentoring program is another area that directly benefits from a diverse team. One way to expand knowledge and influence beyond the mentor/mentee program, and tap into the uniqueness of each person, is through the use of *Mentoring Teams*. These teams are comprised of the leadership team members, the assigned mentors, and other staff who can add value to the conversation regarding the components of your program, how things are going, and what changes need to be made.

This creates opportunities for different individuals, some who are mentors and others who are not, to connect with those within the mentorship program, to add value to one another, and to grow as teachers and leaders. For example, if the school is focused on a literacy initiative, the team may add an instructional literacy specialist to the conversation for technical expertise. One primary reason for having the *Mentoring Teams* in place is to support the mentors.

The meetings are meant to support their growth and development while at the same time building a better program with even more mentors ready to serve in the future. The secondary reason is simply to bring all of the mentors, mentees, and other teacher leaders together to solve common problems in a social way. This type of social problem solving through the use of a diverse team is exciting and energizing.

To be able to mentor effectively, the program should develop these teams to connect with the mentees in orchestrated and structured ways. *Mentoring Teams* should not only represent the staff and the demographic makeup of the school, they should consist of other team members who are not mentors or mentees. The more diversity in the group, the faster and greater the problem solving will be. To foster these relationships and tap into the collective knowledge and skill set of the *Mentoring Teams*, schools can develop *Mentoring Socials*.

Mentoring Socials empower mentors and mentees by having them identify the topic of discussion, which can be specific or general. These socials are after school and designed to be refreshing and engaging. They provide a time for discussions that include the voices of all of the mentees, the mentors, and outside guests who are not "officially" involved in the program.

This concept combines the ideas of the *Social Committee* and *New Teacher Monthly Meetings* from our Accelerated School Acclimation Program (ASAP.) from the last chapter. The twist is that *Mentoring Socials* include all mentees and mentors along with outside guests with the purpose of tackling problems that are identified by mentors. Recall that the *Social Committee* is for new teacher social acclimation and for fun in general, and *New Teacher Monthly Meetings* are facilitated by teacher leaders using school-based topics (more as a teaching tool for new teachers). *Mentoring Socials* are driven by topics of mentoring that *mentors* feel are important for both mentees and themselves. Outside guests are invited to join the fun and/or to address a specific topic as subject matter experts. All three structures are important.

Let's descend into the particulars of the leadership team activity, which is for your leadership team to plan and execute the *Mentoring Socials*. The social should be roughly one hour in length and should include time to develop rapport as well as time to learn with and from one another. The socials can be scripted in various ways, but the first ten to fifteen minutes should always be set up for networking. At events like this, people tend to gravitate to the people they already know. For this reason, we suggest using an icebreaker strategy. For example, each person can choose a strip of paper with a letter on it. The mentors, mentees, guests, and teacher leaders all select a slip of paper. Once everyone has a slip of paper with a letter on it, they find their partner and form pairs. Bs partner with Bs, As get together, and so on. This can be done in a number of ways, but it forces people to move around the room and visit with folks they might not know (or know well).

This networking session is not only a "get to know you" activity, it is set up to begin discussion of the topics that the mentors submitted. It acts as a warm-up. Common topics may include how to reflect together after observing, advice on calling home to parents, how to use technology effectively, or tips for managing time to visit one another. The topics vary, but the goal is that the first few minutes of the social are set aside for the group to listen and learn from one another as a support for the mentoring program. The objective is for everyone to have time to share in a cathartic and safe space.

The bulk of the time thereafter is then organized as a Socratic seminar-style meeting that discusses the topics at hand. We find that this space allows for mentees, who may be in their second or third year of teaching, to add their unique perspective and even play the role of mentor to some degree. The concept of "reverse mentoring" comes to life—a way for younger generations to offer valuable input to seasoned professionals in an informal mentoring capacity (Jordan & Sorell, 2019). As the discussion progresses, it permits everyone in attendance to offer thoughts, forming bonds that will last beyond the social.

The last ten minutes of the social hour is to serve as a time for key takeaways, which essentially consists of the nuggets of information and advice that can truly make a difference for everyone, no matter their years of experience on the team. One facilitator reviews the takeaways, asking for clarity from everyone else. Strategies, like developing *Mentoring Teams*, are critical to the success of any acclimation or mentoring program. When coupled with other aspects of your ASAP, they make the difference for both the leaders, who do the bulk of the planning, and the new teachers on your team. They work as both a motivation and retention plan, and they demonstrate the level of commitment that's needed for mentoring programs, and schools in general, to thrive.

STANDING OUT—WHAT COMMITMENT LOOKS LIKE IN ACTION—CANDICE INNISS

Allows us to introduce Candace Inniss as one of our "standing out" educators. Candace is the epitome of commitment, and her story is an inspiration for all of us. Candace was born in Grenada, what she called "a dot" of an island in the Caribbean. She was raised by her grandmother as her mother traveled back and forth to Caracas, Venezuela, to clean apartments. Eventually, they immigrated to New York where her uncle lived.

As we listened to her story, we could hear the level of commitment she brings to everything she does. With passion and determination, she dedicates herself to the students and to her teammates at Thomas Edison Charter School in Wilmington, where she works as a seventh and eighth grade teacher. But to truly understand Candace, we have to go back to when she was just a teenager.

Candace Inniss moved to Brooklyn, NY, at the age of thirteen, and because of a discrepancy between the US school system and her education in Grenada, she was held back a year and placed in "lower level" courses. She quickly realized that the school assigned her to classes that were below her ability so she worked hard to prove that she was placed in the wrong courses. By the following year, she was in the most challenging programs the school offered. This is where we first see the type of commitment that Candace exudes.

Candace always loved books and reading, and her desire was to become a doctor after high school. She was at the top of her class and graduated as the valedictorian. She mentioned that the valedictorian from her school wasn't just the student with the best grades. It meant she volunteered, played sports, and earned her way into the top ten students of her graduating class. She was drawn to and inspired by a plaque on the wall that named the valedictorian from a previous year. All it took was seeing the recognition bestowed upon another student, and she resolved to do her best in everything that she decided to do.

In the pursuit of her dream as a student of medicine, she quickly realized that she didn't want to be a doctor. She switched majors and earned degrees in both political science and sociology, and set out to join AmeriCorps after graduation. She was assigned to a middle school with a "difficult student population," and that's where she fell in love with teaching. She soon found herself back in school, earning a master's of science in teaching and, through her commitment, she was quickly in front of her own middle school classroom in Brooklyn. She remained there until her family moved to Delaware.

In Delaware, Candace searched for a good fit for what she desired in a school. She went to several job interviews, and then found Thomas Edison Charter School in Wilmington, DE. There was a connection and the school offered her a fifth grade teaching position, which she accepted despite truly wanting to teach at the middle school level. She described her first year or so at Thomas Edison as "turmoil," and she almost left until a new principal, Salome Thomas-EL joined the team. It was her second year when Salome arrived, and it was the turning point for Inniss and the school.

An experienced leader, Salome held a meeting with every teacher to talk about the vision for the future of Edison. In Candace's one-on-one with Salome, something told her to hang in there. Even though she considered leaving, she decided to give it another chance because of a revitalized determination and focus that she felt would make the school a different place. In one short meeting, Edison's new principal convinced her to stay. She said that he really listened to the teachers. "Usually they come on board and bring their own team," she said, but he was different.

Candace wanted to be back at the middle school level, which she told Salome. Without hesitation, he assigned her to the eighth grade. Salome created leadership positions and a team of teacher leaders to support all of the school's unique needs; Candace was the best fit for the Junior Academy Lead Teacher. In this role, she models best practices for other teachers, and she also mentors, helps to acclimate new staff, and acts as a liaison between the administration and the teachers.

Eleven years later, Candace is still at Thomas Edison Charter. She says that "passion is required because our students have a lot going in their lives." She calls it a privilege to serve, and knows that she's on a committed team that has in-depth conversations about what each student needs. They consider best practices to be *per child* not *per classroom* or *per school*.

"We don't all teach the same subjects but we do all teach the same students," she says, which is why it's so important for the teachers and leaders to be on the same page. They conduct morning meetings with homeroom competitions for fun, all of which is teacher-driven. The administration invites new ideas and then supports the teachers in every way, which is one reason she stays at Edison. It is the autonomy that teachers have plus the support that makes the school work. Commitment and mentorship are two-way supports; school leaders are committed to the teachers and the teachers are committed to the school.

Candace Inniss found her niche, and she's especially excited to be contributing to a community of learners "that look like me," as she puts it. She talked about the diverse backgrounds of the students, but she made a particular point about students of color seeing teachers of color as leaders and community advocates.

Candace is making a difference, standing out within our profession, and she contributes because the school environment at Thomas Edison Charter embraces her skills and abilities beyond the classroom. She's a dedicated teacher, but she's also a leader in her school, and her commitment is reciprocated in a way that inspires her to do the work which, in turn, inspires other teachers to do the same. A winning team motivates the players so that their work is impactful, creating momentum for the present and the future. That's the definition of retention at work.

GUIDING QUESTIONS

1. How well does your mentoring program work to develop the skills that new teachers need to be successful?
2. How can you shift your practice to be more deliberate about assigning mentors to mentees?
3. How might you use structures, like *Mentoring Teams* and *Mentoring Socials*, to create support systems for mentors?

Chapter Seven

Conclusion

Cultivating a Membership Mentality

Everything we do, from the moment we meet prospective candidates to the moment they depart as alumni, shapes their membership experience, and with it the very fabric our network (Dignan, 2019, p. 140).

Although the conversation about workplace culture being the driver for employee commitment, contribution, and retention is nothing new, it does require continual attention and focus. Organizational dynamics and bountiful leadership lessons have emerged from the business sector and can be woven meaningfully into the concept of developing *school* culture and overall success within the educational realm. These ideas have permeated the discussion of school leadership for many years and we are excited to blend the two—business and education—for significant gains and recognizable growth.

With this background knowledge and understanding, it's time that we push the boundaries for what we mean when we say "cultivating a positive culture" as school and district leaders. What we've described in this book is a new way of experiencing your school as a teacher; it's a new way to approach culture from both an employer and employee standpoint.

We began this conversation in our book, *Building a Winning Team*, which dives deep into what it means to develop a magnetic reputation with an ability to attract top talent in every school. We see the hiring process as a *before*, *during*, and *after* strategy—you have to set the stage by telling your school's story and by recruiting teachers with an intense program for hiring. Then, and only then, will you be bringing them into a culture of acceptance, growth, and retention. Too often, we divorce hiring from culture, but hiring and retention *are* culture. They come together to complete the picture when it comes to organizational success.

When all of the correct cultural pieces are put into place, similar to a puzzle, schools develop a sense of membership and are far more than just a place of work. Instead of reinforcing the ambiguity of a "positive school culture," we must shift our thinking toward the creation of a "membership mentality" where people feel a sense of accomplishment, praise, purpose, energy, and belonging, from the time they start until the time they relinquish their responsibilities.

We introduced you to the *Retention Accelerators*—motivation, inspiration, and energy. When all three are at play in your organization, you will begin to see the difference in how people interact with one another. We start our membership mentality by ensuring that people have what they need to do their work effectively—the tools to engage and the growth experiences needed to be agile experts. Next we fold *Intrinsic Empowerment* into the membership mentality mix. People need to be empowered by their purpose and embrace the uniqueness of each day rather than simply working toward an arbitrary endpoint. We achieve this by celebrating, praising, and lifting people, concentrating on how they *feel*, not just what they *know* and *do*.

That brings us to the "glue" of every great culture, which is the way we interact with others. Through candor, connections, competence, and courage, we solidify deep relationships throughout the organization as we support and inspire each other. Inspirational leaders are not born; inspiring people is a skill that must be practiced and developed. Leaders who learn to inspire accept this as a key responsibility.

Our roles as leaders become that much more inspiring when our organization is an *H3 Giving School*, a place of generosity and social connectedness. We navigate through our *Professional Purpose Process* and we ward off negativity that can trap our efforts, stifle growth, and stunt progress. We tap into our energy sources, delegating important tasks and modeling what we expect, taking ownership to a new level with our OWN IT model.

Finally, we turn to major support for new people on the team. If we want the future of our profession to be bright, we need the newest members of the workforce to be strong and willing. Better onboarding and quality mentors are needed as we lift educators from day-one. All of this can be a reality through practical application and teamwork. These are the tips, skills, and tools required to transform your culture into a place of membership and belonging. We make changes to professional practices within the school for better retention—better retention means the right people are doing the most important work and, in turn, the school continually evolves into a powerful place of teaching and learning.

As we come to a close, we want to point you toward what we see as the future of this work, pockets of excellence and new thinking that will harness the power of the *Retention Accelerators* and provide hope for our next generation of teachers and leaders. We leave you with the following three concepts (and people doing the work) not just as examples but as models to motivate, inspire, and energize you to do something different and new as well.

First, if you haven't heard Jonathan Alsheimer's message about "Next-Level Teaching," you're missing out. He's a current (as we write this book) classroom teacher with great style and pizzazz. He tells listeners that our purpose as teachers is to empower the students. His voice reverberates as he communicates a new vision for the next level of the profession. "Teach like it's your daughter in the first row." Kids learn fractions because they love their teacher, not the other way around. By the time you're reading this, you can likely pick up a copy of *Next-Level Teaching* to learn what it means to take your classroom to the next level. You can connect by following him on Twitter @mr_Alsheimer.

Second, Suzy Brooks and Matthew Joseph wrote a book called *Modern Mentor*. This new spin on mentorship is all about a collaborative culture with peer mentors and better preparation through on-the-job impact. The authors specifically address the need for teacher job satisfaction and retention. Traditional programming emphasizes content knowledge and philosophical beliefs. The modern mentor changes the focus toward shared accountability and a commitment to one another. You can learn more by following @SimplySuzy and @MatthewXJoseph on Twitter.

Third, our friend Jeanne Wolz runs new teacher mastermind groups. We can't think of a better tool that combines all three of the *Retention Accelerators* than mastermind groups for teachers, especially new and hungry professionals. Jeanne brings together new teachers from across disciplines and grade levels. They discuss new teacher pressure points, provide support for one another, and bring to light best practices at the early stages of their career. Every new teacher deserves a mastermind group. You can contact Jeanne by visiting her website: teacheroffduty.com.

As you can see through just these three examples, the desire and know-how to revolutionize schools is here. The future of teaching and learning is now and the ability to connect with other educators to fuel a grassroots bottom-up movement is within us and upon us. The culture is shifting and transforming the topography of our profession as we speak. Despite the magnitude of the change and the massive working parts involved, there are too many powerful driving forces in motion to stop it from happening. We hope that you'll join us as we embark on a new era of educational leadership and learning, discovering what it means to be motivated, inspired, and energized in schools. As you build your winning team and retain your top talent, we hope to hear from you to add to these stories and many more.

References

Achor, S. (2010). *The happiness advantage: How a positive brain fuels success in work and life*. New York: Crown Publishing Group.

Alliance for Excellent Education. (2004). *Tapping the potential: Retaining and developing high quality teachers*. Washington, DC: Author.

Alsheimer, J. (2020). *Next-level teaching: Empowering students and transforming school culture*. San Diego: Dave Burgess Consulting.

Amazon Jobs. (2019). Retrieved from https://www.amazon.jobs/en/job_catego ries/fulfillment-operations-management?offset=0&result_limit=10&sort =relevant&category=fulfillment-operations-management&distanceType =Mi&radius=24km&latitude=&longitude=&loc_group_id=&loc_query =&base_query=&city=&country=&region=&county=&query_options=&.

Ariely, D. (2016). *Payoff: The hidden logic that shapes our motivations*. New York: Simon & Schuster.

Behrstock-Sherratt, E., Bassett, K., Olson, D., & Jacques, C. (2014). From good to great: Exemplary teachers share perspectives on increasing teacher effectiveness across the career continuum. Center on Great Teachers and Leaders: Air. Retrieved from https://www.air.org/sites/default/files/downloads /report/Exemplary%20Teachers%20Share%20Perspectives%20on%20 Teacher%20Effectiveness_revised.pdf.

Brandau, K., & Ross, D. (2018). *How to earn the gift of discretionary effort*. US: Life Power.

Brooks, S., & Joseph, M. (2019). *Modern mentor: Reimagining mentorship in education*. Highland Heights, OH: Times 10 Publications.

Brown, B. (2018). *Dare to lead: Brave work. Tough conversations. Whole hearts*. New York: Penguin Random House.

Buckingham, M., & Goodall, A. (2019). The feedback fallacy. *Harvard Business Review*. Retrieved from https://hbr.org/2019/03/the-feedback-fallacy.

Byford, M., Watkins, M., & Triantogiannis, L. (2017). Onboarding isn't enough. *Harvard Business Review*. Retrieved from https://hbr.org/2017/05/onboarding-isnt-enough.

Cable, D. (2018). *Alive at work: The neuroscience of helping your people love what they do.* Boston: Harvard Business Review.

Caprino, K. (2012, September 25). What it really takes to be inspiring. Forbes. Retrieved from https://www.forbes.com/sites/kathycaprino/2012/09/25/what-it-really-takes-to-be-inspiring/#6d6a2ded2edf.

Carucci, R. (2018, December 3). To retain new hires, spend more time onboarding them. *Harvard Business Review*. Retrieved from https://hbr.org/2018/12/to-retain-new-hires-spend-more-time-onboarding-them.

Carver-Thomas, D., & Darling-Hammond, L. (2017). *Teacher turnover: Why it matters and what we can do about it.* Palo Alto, CA: Learning Policy Institute.

Casas, J. (2017). *Culturize: Every student. Every day. Whatever it takes.* San Diego: Burgess.

Children's Hospital of Philadelphia (2013, October 21). *Poverty more damaging than gestational drug exposure.* Retrieved from https://www.chop.edu/news/poverty-more-damaging-gestational-drug-exposure.

Chopra, V., & Saint, S. (2017, March 29). 6 things every mentor should do. *Harvard Business Review*. Retrieved from https://hbr.org/2017/03/6-things-every-mentor-should-do.

Clark, R. (2015). *Move your bus: An extraordinary new approach to accelerating success in work and life.* New York: Touchstone.

Collins, J. (2001). *Good to great: Why some companies make the leap . . . and others don't.* New York: HarperCollins Publishers, Inc.

Covey, S. M. R., & Merrill, R. R. (2006). *The speed of trust: The one thing that changes everything.* New York: Free Press.

Covey, S. R. (1993). *The seven habits of highly effective people: Powerful lessons in personal change.* New York: Simon & Schuster.

Coyle, D. (2018). *The culture code: The secrets of highly successful groups.* New York: Penguin Random House.

Crowley, M. C. (2011). *Lead from the heart: Transformational leadership for the 21st century.* Bloomington, IN: Balboa Press.

Dale Carnegie Training. (2011). *Make yourself unforgettable: How to become the person everyone remembers and no one can resist.* New York: Simon & Schuster.

Davis, K. (2018). *Brave leadership: Unleash your most confident, powerful, and authentic self to get the results you need.* Austin: Greenleaf.

Deci, E. L. (1996). *Why we do what we do: Understanding self-motivation.* New York: Penguin.

DesMarais, C. (2016). "Why micromanaging is the worst thing you can do." Inc. Retrieved from https://www.inc.com/christina-desmarais/4-ways-micro managing-will-kill-a-business.html.

Dickens, C. (1843). *A Christmas carol.* London: Chapman & Hall.

Dignan, A. (2019). *Brave new work: Are you ready to reinvent your organization?* New York: Penguin.

Dutton, J. (2003). *Energize your workplace: How to create and sustain high-quality connections at work.* San Francisco: Jossey Bass.

Ellis, A. M., Nifadkar, S. S., Bauer, T. N., and Erdogan, B. (2017, June 20). Your new hires won't succeed unless you onboard them properly. *Harvard Business Review.* Retrieved from https://hbr.org/2017/06/your-new-hires-wont-succeed-unless-you-onboard-them-properly.

Feiman-Nemser, S. (2001). "Helping novices learn to teach." *Journal of Teacher Education,* Vol. 52, No. 1, January/February, 17–30.

Fisher, A. (2018, September 27). This is the top reason people quit their jobs—it's not money. Fortune. Retrieved April 1, 2019, from http://fortune.com/2018/09/27/bored-at-work-why-people-quit-jobs/.

Fleming, A. (2016). The key to adaptable companies is relentlessly developing people. *Harvard Business Review.* Retrieved from https://hbr.org/2016/10/the-key-to-adaptable-companies-is-relentlessly-developing-people.

Frederickson, B. (2019). Leading with positive emotions. Michigan Ross. Retrieved from https://www.bus.umich.edu/facultyresearch/research/Trying Times/PositiveEmotions.htm.

Fullan, M. (2014). *The principal: The keys to maximizing impact.* San Francisco: Jossey-Bass.

———. (2019). *Nuance: Why some leaders succeed and others fail.* Thousand Oaks, CA: Corwin.

Fullan, M., & Quinn, J. (2016). *Coherence: The right drivers in action for schools, districts, and systems.* Thousand Oaks, CA: Sage.

Fuller, R., & Shikaloff, N. (2017, February 16). Being engaged at work is not the same as being productive. *Harvard Business Review.* Retrieved from https://hbr.org/2017/02/being-engaged-at-work-is-not-the-same-as-being-productive.

Garton, E. (2017). The case for investing more in people. *Harvard Business Review.* Retrieved from https://hbr.org/2017/09/the-case-for-investing-more-in-people.

Garton, E., & Mankins, M. (2015, December 9). Engaging your employees is good, but don't stop there. *Harvard Business Review.* Retrieved from https://hbr.org/2015/12/engaging-your-employees-is-good-but-dont-stop-there.

Gino, F. (2018). *Rebel talent: Why it pays to break the rules at work and in life.* New York: HarperCollins.

Godin, S. (2010). *Linchpin: Are you indispensable?* New York: Penguin.

Goldrick, L. (2016). Support from the start: A 50-state review of policies on new educator induction and mentoring. New Teacher Center Policy Report. Retrieved from https://newteachercenter.org/wp-content/uploads/2016Comp leteReportStatePolicies.pdf.

Goler, L., Gale, J., Harrington, B., and Grant, A. (2018, January 11). Why people really quit their jobs. *Harvard Business Review.* Retrieved from https://hbr.org/2018/01/why-people-really-quit-their-jobs.

Gordon, J. (2012). *The positive dog: A story about the power of positivity.* New York: John Wiley & Sons.

———. (2018). *The power of a positive team: Proven principles and practices that make great teams great.* Hoboken, NJ: John Wiley & Sons.

Gostick, A., & Elton, C. (2007). *The carrot principle: How the best managers use recognition to engage their people, retain talent, and accelerate performance.* New York: Free Press.

Guha, R., Hyler, M. E., and Darling-Hammond, L. (2016). *The teacher residency: An innovative model for preparing teachers.* Palo Alto, CA: Learning Policy Institute.

Hadeed, K. (2017). *Permission to screw up: How I learned to lead by doing (almost) everything wrong.* New York: Penguin Random House.

Hallowell, E. M. (2011). *Shine: Using brain science to get the best from your people.* Boston: Harvard Business Review.

Hart, W. E. (2010). Seven ways to be an effective mentor. Forbes. Retrieved from https://www.forbes.com/2010/06/30/mentor-coach-executive-training -leadership-managing-ccl.html#1fa1739a3fd3.

Hattie, J. (2009). *Visible learning: A synthesis of over 800 meta-analyses relating to achievement.* London: Routledge.

Hedges, K. (2017). *The inspiration code: How the best leaders energize people every day.* New York: American Management Association.

Hess, F. (2013). *Cage-busting leadership.* Cambridge, MA: Harvard Education.

Hill, L. A., & Lineback, K. (2011). Are you a good boss—or a great one? *Harvard Business Review.* Retrieved from https://hbr.org/2011/01/are-you -a-good-boss-or-a-great-one.

Horwitch, M., & Whipple, M. (2014, June 11). Leaders who inspire: A 21st-century approach to developing your talent. Bain & Company. Retrieved from https://www.bain.com/insights/leaders-who-inspire.

Ingersoll, R., & Strong, M. (2011). The impact of induction and mentoring programs for beginning teachers: A critical review of the research. Penn Libraries. Retrieved from https://repository.upenn.edu/cgi/viewcontent.cgi ?article=1127&context=gse_pubs.

Jaffe, R., & Taylor, W. (2018). *The physics of energy*. New York: Cambridge University Press.

Johnson, S. M., Berg, J. H., & Donaldson, M. L. (2005). *Who stays in teaching and why? A review of the literature on teacher retention*. Washington, DC: National Retired Teachers Association.

Johnson, W. (2018). How to lose your best employees. *Harvard Business Review*. Retrieved from https://hbr.org/2018/04/how-to-lose-your-best-employees.

Johnson, W. B., & Smith, D. G. (2018). The best mentors think like Michelangelo. *Harvard Business Review*. Retrieved from https://hbr.org/2018/01/the-best-mentors-think-like-michelangelo.

Jones, J., & Vari, T. (2019). *Candid and compassionate feedback: Transforming everyday practice in schools*. New York: Routledge.

Jordan, J., & Sorell, M., (2019). Why you should create a "shadow board" of younger employees. *Harvard Business Review*. Retrieved from https://hbr.org/2019/06/why-you-should-create-a-shadow-board-of-younger-employees.

Kelada, I. (2018). *21 days to happiness: Increase your happiness, productivity and energy*. Wellness Ink.

Khan Academy (2017, May 8). Studying for the SAT for 20 hours on Khan Academy associated with 115-point average score increase. Retrieved from https://www.khanacademy.org/about/blog/post/160451329150/studying-for-the-sat-for-20-hours-on-khan-academy.

Kislik, L. (2018, September 19). How to retain and engage your B players. *Harvard Business Review*. Retrieved from https://hbr.org/2018/09/how-to-retain-and-engage-your-b-players.

Klinghoffer, D., Young, C., & Liu, X. (2018, June 14). To retain new hires, make sure you meet with them in their first week. *Harvard Business Review* Retrieved from https://hbr.org/2018/06/to-retain-new-hires-make-sure-you-meet-with-them-in-their-first-week.

Knight, R. (2015, August 21). How to stop micromanaging your team. *Harvard Business Review*. Retrieved from https://hbr.org/2015/08/how-to-stop-micromanaging-your-team.

Mankins, M. C., & Garton, E. (2017). *Time, talent, energy: Overcome organizational drag and unleash your team's productive power*. Boston: Harvard Business Review.

Maxwell, J. (1998). *The 21 irrefutable laws of leadership: Follow them and people will follow you*. Nashville: Thomas Nelson.

Maxwell, J. (2012). *The 15 invaluable laws of growth*. New York: Hachette.

McFeely, S. (2018). Why your best teachers are leaving and 4 ways to keep them. Gallup Education. Retrieved from https://www.gallup.com/education/237275/why-best-teachers-leaving-ways-keep.aspx.

McKee, A. (2018). *How to be happy at work: The power of purpose, hope, and friendship*. Boston: Harvard Business Review.

Mechlinski, J. (2018). *Shift the work: The revolutionary science of moving from apathetic to all in using your head, heart, and gut.* New York: Morgan James.

Murad, A. (2014, May 1). How to ask for help at work without looking bad. FOXBusiness. Retrieved from https://www.foxbusiness.com/features/how-to-ask-for-help-at-work-without-looking-bad.

Nemours. (2009). Standards of behavior. Retrieved from https://www.nemours.org/content/dam/nemours/www/filebox/healthpro/medstaff/behavior.pdf.

O'Hara, C. (2014, August 27). Who's being left out on your team? *Harvard Business Review*. Retrieved from https://hbr.org/2014/08/whos-being-left-out-on-your-team.

Patterson, K., Grenny, J., Maxfield, D., McMillan, R., & Switzler, A. (2008). *Influencer: The power to change anything.* New York: McGraw-Hill.

Pink, D. (2009). *Drive: The surprising truth about what motivates us.* New York: Riverhead.

Plato. (n.d.). *The Republic, Book I.* Retrieved from https://oregonstate.edu/instruct/phl201/modules/Philosophers/Plato/republic_book_one.pdf.

Podolsky, A., Kini, T., Bishop, J., & Darling-Hammond, L. (2016). *Solving the teacher shortage: How to attract and retain excellent educators.* Palo Alto, CA: Learning Policy Institute.

Rowley, J. B. (1999). The good mentor. ASCD. Retrieved from http://www.ascd.org/publications/educational-leadership/may99/vol56/num08/The-Good-Mentor.aspx.

Schaffhauser, D. (2014, July 17). *The problem isn't teacher recruiting; it's retention.* THEJournal. Retrieved from https://thejournal.com/articles/2014/07/17/the-problem-isnt-teacher-recruiting-its-retention.aspx.

Schwantes, M. (2018, December 21). *Why do employees quit on their bosses? Because of 5 common reasons still not addressed, says new research.* Inc. Retrieved from https://www.inc.com/marcel-schwantes/why-do-people-quit-their-jobs-exactly-new-research-points-finger-at-5-common-reasons.html.

Schwartz, T. (2012, January 23). Why appreciation matters so much. *Harvard Business Review*. Retrieved from https://hbr.org/2012/01/why-appreciation-matters-so-mu.

Scott, K. (2017). *Radical candor: Be a kick-ass boss without losing your humanity.* New York: St. Martin's.

Sutcher, Darling-Hammond, L., and Carver-Thomas, D. (2016). A coming crisis in teaching? Teacher supply, demand, and shortages in the U.S. Learning Policy Institute. Retrieved from https://learningpolicyinstitute.org/product/coming-crisis-teaching.

Tate, C. (2017). *The purpose project.* Carolyn Tate & Co.

Thomas-EL, S., Jones, J., & Vari, T. (2020). *Passionate leadership: Creating a culture of success in every school.* Thousand Oaks, CA: Corwin.

Tjan, A. K. (2017). What the best mentors do. *Harvard Business Review*. Retrieved from https://hbr.org/2017/02/what-the-best-mentors-do.

Whitaker, T. (2012). *What great principals do differently: Eighteen things that matter most*. New York: Routledge.

———. (2014). *Shifting the monkey: The art of protecting good people from liars, criers, and other slackers (A book on school leadership and teacher performance)*. Bloomington, IN: Triple Nickel.

———. (2015). *Dealing with difficult teachers*. New York: Routledge.

Willink, J., & Babin, L. (2015). *Extreme ownership: How U.S. Navy SEALs lead and win*. New York: St. Martin's.

Wooden, J., & Jamison, S. (2005). *Wooden on leadership: How to create a winning organization*. New York: McGraw-Hill.

Yokoyama, J., & Michelli, J. (2004). *When fish fly: Lessons for creating a vital and energized workplace from the world famous Pike Place Fish Market*. New York: Hyperion.

About the Authors

Dr. Joseph Jones is the superintendent of the New Castle County Vocational-Technical School District in Delaware. Joe is a former high school social studies teacher, assistant principal, and principal. As principal, he was named the Delaware Secondary Principal of the Year and during his tenure, Delcastle Technical High School was the first high school to receive the state's Outstanding Academic Achievement Award. He received his doctorate from the University of Delaware in educational leadership and was awarded the outstanding doctoral student award of his class. Currently, Joe works closely with local and state leaders on student achievement and accountability and has spearheaded an aggressive and successful campaign to ensure student success. Joe is also an adjunct professor, teaching and designing curriculum, both at the undergraduate and graduate levels, for various universities. He presents nationally on topics of school leadership and is the cofounder of the leadership development institute, TheSchoolHouse302. Along with T.J. Vari, he coauthored *Candid and Compassionate Feedback: Transforming Everyday Practice in Schools*. And, with Salome Thomas-EL and T.J. Vari, he coauthored *Passionate Leadership: Creating a Culture of Success in Every School* as well as *Building a Winning Team: The Power of a Magnetic Reputation and the Need to Recruit Top Talent in Every School*.

Dr. Salome Thomas-EL has been a teacher and principal in Philadelphia, PA, and Wilmington, DE, since 1987. He is currently the head of school at Thomas Edison Charter School in Wilmington, DE.

Thomas-EL received national acclaim as a teacher and chess coach at Roberts Vaux Middle School, where his students have gone on to win world recognition as eight-time National Chess Champions. Principal EL was a regular contributor on the *Dr. Oz Show* and the author of the best-selling books, *I Choose to Stay* and *The Immortality of Influence (Foreword by Will Smith)*. The Walt Disney Company optioned the movie rights to *I Choose to Stay*. Thomas-EL speaks to groups across the country and frequently appears on C-SPAN, CNN, and NPR. He has received the Marcus Foster Memorial Award for Administrator Excellence as a school district administrator in Philadelphia and the University of Pennsylvania's distinguished Martin Luther King Jr. Community Involvement Award. *Reader's Digest* magazine recognized Principal EL as an "Inspiring American Icon" and he has appeared on *Oprah Radio*. And, with Joseph Jones and T.J. Vari, he coauthored *Passionate Leadership: Creating a Culture of Success in Every School* as well as *Building a Winning Team: The Power of a Magnetic Reputation and the Need to Recruit Top Talent in Every School*.

Dr. T.J. Vari is the assistant superintendent of secondary schools and district operations in the Appoquinimink School District in Delaware. He is a former middle school assistant principal and principal, and a former high school English teacher and department chair. His master's degree is in school leadership and his doctorate is in innovation and leadership where he accepted an Award for Academic Excellence given to one doctoral student per graduating class. He holds several honors and distinctions, including his past appointment as president of the Delaware Association of School Administrators, his work with the Delaware Association of School Principals, and the honor in accepting the Paul Carlson Administrator of the Year Award. His efforts span beyond the K–12 arena into higher education where he holds adjunct appointments, teaching courses at the master's and doctoral level. He is a national presenter on topics of school leadership and the cofounder of TheSchoolHouse302, a leadership development institute. Along with Joseph Jones, he coauthored *Candid and Compassionate Feedback: Transforming Everyday Practice in Schools*. And, with Salome Thomas-EL and Joseph Jones, he coauthored *Passionate Leadership: Creating a Culture of Success in Every School* as well as *Building a Winning Team: The Power of a Magnetic Reputation and the Need to Recruit Top Talent in Every School*.